SpringerBriefs in Computer Science

T0235667

Series Editors

Stan Zdonik

Peng Ning

Shashi Shekhar

Jonathan Katz

Xindong Wu

Lakhmi C. Jain

David Padua

Xuemin Shen

Borko Furht

V. S. Subrahmanian

Martial Hebert

Katsushi Ikeuchi

Bruno Siciliano

For further volumes:
http://www.springer.com/series/10028

Maurizio Martellini
Editor

Cyber Security

Deterrence and IT Protection for Critical Infrastructures

 Springer

Editor
Maurizio Martellini
Landau Network Centro Volta/ICIS
Como
Italy

ISSN 2191-5768   ISSN 2191-5776   (electronic)
ISBN 978-3-319-02278-9   ISBN 978-3-319-02279-6   (eBook)
DOI 10.1007/978-3-319-02279-6
Springer Cham Heidelberg New York Dordrecht London

Library of Congress Control Number: 2013949244

Printed on acid-free paper

Springer is part of Springer Science+Business Media (www.springer.com)

Preface

The recent years have been characterized by an increase in cyber attacks against sovereign states' critical infrastructures, government offices, and economic institutions, whether they have been attacks oriented to the control of the infrastructure (such as Stuxnet, the computer virus which infected computers controlling uranium enrichment facilities in Iran in 2010) or to espionage and the theft of confidential data (such as Flame, a malware discovered in 2012, used for targeted cyber espionage in Middle Eastern countries). For this reason cyber security is becoming one of the pivotal challenges that governments are called to face today, as systems that constitute the core of modern society, economy, and defense are empowered by information technology (IT). It goes without saying that IT has provided, and is still providing, enormous benefits in terms of communication, productivity, and wellbeing, but at the same time a holistic and analytical approach to prevent, identify, and respond quickly to cyber attacks is needed.

Indeed, the aforementioned cases are practical examples that cyber attacks are not anymore bound to a limited scale and that the critical nature of targets is increasing. With it, the potential for harmful consequences on civil society is also increasing. Cyber attacks are undoubtedly a new weapon in the hands of both governments and non-state actors, because they provide low-cost means of exploiting vulnerabilities found in most computer networks that run critical infrastructures including power plants and grids; utility pipelines; transportation; or laboratories handling chemical, biological, radiological or nuclear (CBRN) materials. In addition to that, international doctrines for deterrence and defense against cyber attacks are just developing and only in some cases are being assimilated in national and international defense complexes. Without entering into the merits of the problem of attribution, it seemed clear in 2010 that state actors were behind both the Stuxnet malware and its attack against the Natanz uranium enrichment facility, and other attacks discovered afterwards, i.e., Flame and Duqu (a malware similar to Stuxnet, but with the task of collecting information). The implications here regarding the cyber space and cyber deterrence are very strong. For the first time in history—after years of computer viruses that led only to minor malfunctioning and data loss-malwares hit SCADA Systems (Supervisory Control And Data Acquisition, which are industrial control systems for monitoring and managing industrial infrastructure or facility-based processes), resulting in the physical tampering of a nation state's critical infrastructure.

Before 2010, assessment of cyber attacks was generally that they are limited in scale, carried out by private actors, and without a specific target. In this light, the above quoted examples were game-changers and draw attention to main actors that are now nations using outright cyber weapons and being able to cause physical disruption of systems. The infamous malwares were the clear example of what a nation state is capable of and willing to achieve with cyber weapons. Another important implication for international security that Stuxnet brought to light to the global audience was the serious problem of the so-called Zero-Day Exploits (ZDE). A ZDE is a malicious code that exploits one or more vulnerabilities in the system that no one is aware of; consequently, this means that no defense exists for such unknown weaknesses. The fact that antivirus softwares cannot detect ZDEs helps the virus(es) to remain concealed and working in the shadows. For example, Stuxnet used four Zero-Day Exploits (defining an unusual high complexity) that couldn't be detected by security experts that, together with the ability of the malware to hide the modifications it made, helped to hide its two-years attack aimed at damaging Iranian nuclear infrastructures. Flame, that had the same basic structure as Stuxnet, involved one of the same Zero-Day Exploits that allowed the malware to penetrate the systems, so that it was capable to steal confidential information for five years. Flame, which had not only access to the hard drives of the system, was also able to monitor keystrokes or turn on the microphones of the computers connected to the network, enabling espionage and the theft of confidential information. Another significant implication is that ZDEs can be bought and sold and are highly priced. For this reason governments (and businesses alike) are becoming more aware of the importance of having highly skilled researchers capable of finding weaknesses and compiling ZDEs, in order not only to attack an enemy's system but also to defend their own. Obviously this at a constantly escalating price both for attacking and for defending, thus creating a vicious circle. As a consequence, one of the main duties of governments, and security and military experts, has become the outlining of a new approach of a comprehensive cyber defense, that encompasses the logic of resilience applied to the cyber world, the imperative need to protect a nation's critical assets, and how to do it. For a good, planned defense, being able to deter an attack is the first step; but it is not enough and critical assets must still be protected against internal and external cyber attacks. This could be reached moving towards a resilience approach that involves the entire establishment of the infrastructure, in order to be able to withstand and, if necessary, recover quickly from a cyber attack.

Some observers believe that development of cyber weapons is following the same path set as when nuclear weapons were first developed. Then, the world was characterized by the phrase "Mutually Assured Destruction," with nuclear testing intended to demonstrate to adversaries the powerful threat presented by nuclear weaponry. However, the treaties among nations that enabled cooperation for controlling the spread of nuclear weapons in the past may not be a useful model for controlling the spread of cyber weapons. Cyber weapons do not have containers that can be counted to measure the level of compliance with treaty rules, and they cannot be openly tested to warn adversaries about the possible magnitude of their destructive capabilities. Finally, when a cyber weapon is released in a cyberattack, after it is discovered and isolated, the targeted nation will actually possess an exact copy of the weapon. This can be reverse engineered, modified, and sent back at a later time to attack the originator of the malicious code. These and other characteristics of cyber weapons make them difficult items to manage through international cooperation for nonproliferation.

Thus, several are the uncertainties and the gray zones around the cyber threat, and providing a comprehensive analysis is not a simple task. This collection of occasional papers—where experts of the International Working Group—Landau Network Centro Volta (IWG-LNCV) discuss aspects of cyber security—tries to present possible methods of deterrence and defense against cyber attacks with a holistic approach.

Contents

Contributors

Sandro Bologna has more than 40 years experience with the Italian National Agency for New Technologies, Energy and Sustainable Economic Development (ENEA) and abroad, where he has covered different positions as Researcher, Head of Research Units, Head of Research Projects at national and international levels. His main research activities deal with the achievement and assessment of computer-based system safety and reliability, large networks vulnerability analysis, critical infrastructure protection, and resilience. e-mail: s.bologna@infrastrutturecritiche.it

Alessandro Fasani collaborates with the LNCV as Project Assistant in the framework of the LNCV Science and Technology for Non-Proliferation Programme. He is interested in international CBRN security and cybersecurity. He holds a BA in Interpreting and Communication from IULM University in Italy and an MA in International Relations from the Catholic University of the Sacred Heart of Milan. e-mail: alessandro.fasani@centrovolta.it

Sandro Gaycken is a researcher in technology and security at the Freie Universität Berlin, Institute of Computer Science. He is a graduate philosopher with a doctorate in technology research. The main focus of his research is on IT and society, involving topics like cybersecurity, cyberwarfare, hacking and hackers, surveillance, open source, information society. In addition to his research, Sandro Gaycken consults security institutions and policy-making bodies at home and abroad as well as companies in the fields of defense and IT. He has testified as a subject-matter expert in many hearings in the Bundestag, in a range of ministries at NATO, the G8, the EU, and other major institutions. e-mail: s.gaycken@fu-berlin.de

Maurizio Martellini is Secretary General of the Landau Network-Centro Volta, Executive Secretary of the International Working Group (IWG), Professor of Physics at the University of Insubria (Como, Italy), and Member of the Pugwash General Conferences. He has published in the fields of international security and physics on specialized journals and authored about a hundred articles on national and international geopolitical/security affairs. He is an advisor to the Italian Ministry of Foreign Affairs. His fields of Research and Analysis are: methods in theoretical and nuclear physics; global issues, global scientists redirection/engagement, management and disposal of radioactive waste; scientific and technological aspects concerning international security, CBRN risks mitigation issues, Cyber security of Critical Infrastructures; Science and Engineering diplomacy. e-mail: Maurizio.martellini@centrovolta.it

Stephanie Meulenbelt obtained an LLM in International Law from the University of Reading, UK and an MA in Criminology from the University of Utrecht, the Netherlands. She has worked for the Organisation for the Prohibition of Chemical Weapons. Currently, she is employed at the Netherlands Organisation for Applied Scientific Research (TNO), where she joined the "CBRN Protection" research group. e-mail: stephanie.meulenbelt@tno.nl

Krzysztof Paturej has been Director, from 2006 to 2013, of the Office of Special Projects in the OPCW Technical Secretariat. Now he is Ambassador Titular at the Ministry of Foreign Affairs of the Republic of Poland. Mr. Paturej is experienced in multilateral diplomacy, negotiations and multicultural relations, disarmament and non-proliferation of WMD, efforts against terrorism, development and cooperation programs, relations with stakeholders and public society, result-based management and risk management strategies. In his recent function at the OPCW, Mr. Paturej is responsible, inter alia, for coordination of the OPCW policies in disarmament, WMD non-proliferation and global efforts against terrorism, relations and programs with the OPWC stakeholders and international partners, and the development of the OPCW policies on prevention of and preparedness for misuse of toxic chemicals and chemical safety and security.e-mail: krzysztof.paturej@msz.gov.pl

Thomas Shea served for 24 years at the International Atomic Energy Agency, leading activities involving safeguards policy, implementation of verification at plutonium processing plants, and development of a verification system for classified forms of fissile material. He later served as Director of Defense Nuclear Nonproliferation Programs at Pacific Northwest National Laboratory and currently is the owner of TomSheaNuclear Consulting Services. Dr. Shea received his Ph.D. in Nuclear Science from Rensselaer Polytechnic Institute. He is a Fellow Emeritus of the Institute of Nuclear Materials Management, a recipient of the INMM Distinguished Service Award, and a member of the international subcommittee of the US Department of Energy Nuclear Energy Advisory Committee. e-mail: tomsheanuclear@me.com

Clay Wilson is the director for the Cybersecurity Policy Program at UMUC, which awards the master's degree and several graduate certificates in cybersecurity policy. In this position, he oversees the curriculum development, and operation of the Capstone Critical Infrastructure Cybersecurity Simulation. He has taught Global Cybersecurity Policy, as well as Cybersecurity and Risk Analysis. Dr. Wilson is a former executive and technology and national defense policy analyst for the Congressional Research Service. He has written reports for the U.S. Congress and NATO committees on net-centric warfare, cybersecurity, nanotechnology, and on vulnerabilities of high-technology military systems and critical infrastructures. e-mail: clay.wilson@umuc.edu

About the IWG-LNCV

The International Working Group (IWG)

The International Working Group was established in November 2001 as an informal forum for discussion, encouraging collaboration and exchanges of ideas and information on policies and projects relating to the human dimension particularly related to scientist engagement activities to be undertaken globally, under the Global Partnership and other related international initiatives. Participants in the IWG assist in the monitoring and facilitating progress of pre-defined projects and programs to enable evaluation and promotion of best practice and lessons learnt to take place effectively. The operation of the IWG Secretariat is entrusted to the Landau Network-Centro Volta (LNCV), Como, Italy. This provides premises and infrastructure necessary for its work. Funding support for the work of the IWG and its Secretariat over the past few years has come from a number of GP countries and the European Commission. World leaders at the L'Aquila G8 summit noted that the threat from proliferation sensitive expertise and information had now largely moved away from Cold War legacy concerns in the Former Soviet Union, to a global one where the potential threats were more diffuse but still embraced CBRN proliferation sensitive expertise. The summit recommended that a more coordinated approach in the field of global WMD knowledge proliferation and scientist engagement should be pursued—to enhance international collaboration and enable it to take place in an effective and more comprehensive manner.

The IWG provides a forum and an "Implementation Working Group" to assist and serve the GP community to progress these recommendations, and importantly, provide a framework to allow for effective monitoring and evaluation of global engagement activities.

Landau Network Centro Volta (LNCV)

The Landau Network-Centro Volta (LNCV), founded in 1995, is a non-profit and non-governmental organization operating as a global network of international experts supporting global security, disarmament, and cooperation. Its programs cover research on international security and policy issues, worldwide disarmament of Weapons of Mass Destruction, arms control, scientific and technologic cooperation for global peace support, water, and energy security.

Cyber as Deterrent

Sandro Gaycken and Maurizio Martellini

Abstract *"Cyber as Deterrent"* authored by Maurizio Martellini and Sandro Gaycken, is a state-of-the-art document on the deterrence power of cyber attacks. It is divided in five parts: the first explains some characteristics relevant to understand the specifics of cybered deterrence; the second one explores possible doctrines of cybered deterrence and their effects; the third one will determine relevant features for the design of a force posture; the fourth analyses the dilemmas stemming from the uncertainty of attribution of an attack, that's to say escalating or refrain from continuing the counterattack; the fifth part compares cybered deterrence and nuclear deterrence, concluding that the basic benchmarks underpinning nuclear deterrence are not effective for cyber warfare, and that "cyber as a deterrent" doesn't seem like a valid tool in comparable situations of serious crisis among states.

Executive Summary

Offensive cyber capabilities can be used as a new and an unconventional kind of deterrent. This chapter will explore some applying conditions and options, in five sections. First, it will sketch out some basics. It will explain some characteristics relevant to understand the specifics of cybered deterrence:

- basic capabilities are cheap and achievable;
- everyone can undertake cybered deterrence;
- high tech nations are more vulnerable, thus prima facie more easily deterred by cyber capabilities;

S. Gaycken (✉)
IWG and Frei Universitat Berlin, Berlin, Germany
e-mail: s.gaycken@fu-berlin.de

M. Martellini
IWG and Landau Network–Centro Volta Como, Como, Italy
e-mail: maurizio.martellini@centrovolta.it

M. Martellini (ed.), *Cyber Security*, SpringerBriefs in Computer Science,
DOI: 10.1007/978-3-319-02279-6_1, © The Author(s) 2013

- cyber attacks can be anonymized or undertaken as false flag operations and:
- cyber attacks can have a high granularity and their effects can be reversible.

The second part will explore possible doctrines of cybered deterrence and their effects:

- a "Targeted Capability" doctrine would demonstrate a mastery to attack only specific systems used in specific military, economical or political actions;
- a "General Capability" doctrine would demonstrate a mastery to attack any kind of system;
- a doctrine of "Assured Disruption" would show an ability to disrupt vital IT-services and data highways;
- a doctrine of "Forced Transparency" would demonstrate an ability to obtain secret information;
- a doctrine of "Silent Erosion" would demonstrate a capability to weaken a society or an economy through a series of indefensible minor events and finally:
- a doctrine of "Digital Media Control" could demonstrate an ability to orchestrate cyber information operations and spin narratives of strategic impact through a use of digital media.

The third part of the piece will determine relevant features for the design of a force posture. Relevant characteristics to determine the quality of a cyber deterrent will be:

- the difficulty of the target chosen and the tasks to be completed;
- the technical heterogeneity of targets and tasks mastered;
- the depth and reach of penetration relative to sophistication of security layering;
- the duration until detection relative to sophistication of sensors;
- the mastery of operation relative to its overall operational complexity;
- the mastery of anonymity and pseudonymity relative to measures of identity enforcement and:
- the overall elegance of design and operation.
- The fourth part of the paper will highlight two dilemmas which might evolve from cybered deterrence:
- uncertainty in the interpretation of an attack might cause unintended escalations and cause nations to choose to refrain from cybered deterrence to avoid escalation or:
- uncertainty about the identity and the intent of an attack might cause defenders to pick up strategic compensation by engaging in offensive cyber attacks themselves, leading to more uncertainty and escalation.

The fifth part of the chapter will compare cybered deterrence and nuclear deterrence, concluding that the basic benchmarks underpinning nuclear deterrence are not effective for cyberwarfare, and that "cyber as a deterrent" doesn't seem like a valid tool in comparable situations of serious crisis among states. However, cybered deterrence offers its very own set of opportunities, and might nonetheless evolve into a new and alternative deterrent posture alongside traditional postures such as nuclear MAD, especially for previously strategically less relevant nations.

Basics of Cybered Deterrence

Cybered deterrence[1] can best be defined as the use of hacking capabilities to threaten to attack an adversary's information technology. As a threat, this might not sound very special at the outset. Ballistic rockets can be used to attack information technology too. But hacking capabilities carry a number of special characteristics which differentiate them from plain kinetic measure.

First of all, cyber deterrence is for everyone. Offensive cyber capabilities are not as difficult to obtain as most other military capabilities. There is a shortness of human resources at present. But getting good hackers is not a problem per se. The knowledge is available. It is not very specific. And it can be taught. So getting the people to do the job will be a question of time rather than a principal concern. Also, hacking capabilities are not expensive. There is little need for costly special technology. Militaries only need the brains to design the attack, an intelligence service for reconnaissance and for the deployment of the attack, and testing equipment, depending on the targets they will aim for. Most of that equipment will be standard IT and readily available for a low price. These basic operational conditions render offensive military hacking easily possible for almost every state (and some larger criminal organizations) in the world.

Second, cybered deterrence primarily affects high tech nations. The more dependent a state is on information technology and the more vulnerable its technology is to hacking, the more credible and the more effective is a threat of military hacking against it. This is what renders offensive cyber warfare particularly interesting for nations which previously were strategically less relevant. Such nations could consider it a strategic equalizer. The dominance of the traditionally strategically relevant nations is mostly based on high tech, IT-based advantages. The ensuing strategic dependence on these IT-advantages, however, can now be turned into a decisive disadvantage. These new players still have to identify a threshold up to which they can threaten high tech, dominant countries with cyber capabilities. The USA and Europe for instance will be very vulnerable to cyber attacks. They are highly dependent upon insecure information technology. But if another state chooses to threaten them with cyber capabilities, they might reply with conventional threats like embargos or kinetic weaponry. Cybered deterrence still has to be considered as a part of a system of deterrents, not in isolation. However, it does lend great power if the threshold on when and how to use it is well-defined. Defining the threshold will depend on numerous factors such as the sensitivity of the victim towards cyber attacks, the political narratives on escalation in-kind or cross-domain, the ability of the attacker to create the right kind of deterrent narrative, his ability to control the extent of collateral damage, the chosen deterrent doctrine, and other things. But there is no doubt that this power could

---

[1] Whenever we speak of "cyber as a deterrent", we will use the term "cybered deterrence" instead of "cyber deterrence" as this latter phrase is commonly used in the context of "deterring cyber".

be used in sub-conflict diplomatic quarrels inasmuch as in times of conflict as a sole or as an additional instrument of pressure.

Third, attribution can be either avoided or directed. The attacker can always choose if he wants to be identified, how he wants to be identified or if he wants someone else to be identified. Normally, attribution of cybered deterrence will not form a problem. It will be guaranteed through conventional communication as a deterring force wants to be identified. However, the option to orchestrate attribution might initiate alternative deterrent strategies. Deterrence does not necessarily require strict identification. An attacker could choose to launch a demonstrative cyber attack to force the victim to withdraw from certain political moves without identifying as the country against which these moves are aimed—the attacker could simply appear as an anonymous, but capable "friend in need". Such deterrence strategies would be rather new, and still have to explored.

Fourth, cyber attacks can have a high granularity, and they can be reversible. These specific characteristics actually render them very attractive for deterrence at large. Deterring moves can be orchestrated with great precision, with very specific effects in very specific areas, and many effects can be reversed, leaving the impression of a capability to do damage without actually having caused any damage.

Doctrines of Cybered Deterrence

If cybered deterrence is picked up as a political tool, the question has to be answered how the deterrence posture is to be designed. Such a posture consists of many elements such as doctrine, force posture, command and control procedures, escalatory models, escalatory narratives, concepts and analysis, or technical and non-technical capabilities. It has to be crafted very carefully to avoid misperceptions and unintended escalation. Many of these elements still remain to be determined and cannot be anticipated reliably. But some of the possible doctrines of cybered deterrence and the conditions for a force posture can be predicted.

The choice of doctrines is comparatively large. This is owed to the fact that cyber activities offer an unusually rich target set, with plenty of tactical options on how to handle it. Some types of doctrines can be considered very likely. They can be used in isolation or in combination.

First, an actor could choose a doctrine of "Targeted Capability". In this case, he would demonstrate only a specific ability to attack very specific systems. Examples could be C4ISR-systems on the battlefield or specific financial software used at stock exchanges. In this case, only specific kinds of activities could be affected, addressing specific kinds of activities and avoiding escalation by being accused of attacking other activities.

Second, a doctrine of "General Capability" could be chosen. This way, an actor would demonstrate a broad ability to hack all kinds of systems. This would function as a more general deterrent, but with a higher likelihood for escalation.

Third, in both of these cases, the actor could choose to demonstrate abilities for specific kinds of attacks. A doctrine of "Assured Disruption" for instance would demonstrate an ability to disrupt vital IT-services or data streams to cause financial and strategic losses. Such an ability could interrupt foreign attacks or simply cause a simple, visible, yet effective damage. A simple disruption of services is not very elegant of course. It is the wooden club in the armory of the cyber soldier. But a very large wooden club will have a deterrent effect nonetheless. The addressee would have to fear for the reliability of IT-based processes in his nation. Such a deterrence doctrine might also force him into expensive investments for redundancies and securities, or even into downgrading these services, thus causing strategic weaknesses.

A doctrine of "Forced Transparency" on the other hand could demonstrate abilities to gather secret information and either keep it, sell it or hand it to the public. Both of these doctrines would have different effects on the addressee. In this case, the addressee would have to expect that anything he does could be known in advance and transmitted to someone else, probably causing the addressee to abandon certain activities he does not wish to be associated with.

Fourth, a doctrine of "Silent Erosion" could be chosen as well. In this case, a deterring actor would demonstrate and communicate the easiest and most worrisome ability among all cyber abilities. He could demonstrate a capability to cause not only single, lightning strikes on critical infrastructures or the like, but rather lots of minor incidents, weakening and slowly eroding the society targeted. Especially if directed against an economy, such a strategy could be almost impossible to defend against and profitable at the same time, thus very attractive at large. In this case, an attacker could steal a lot of intellectual property over a long period of time, and sabotage and outbid the original products. Such an ability might have good deterrent effects. Adversaries would have to live with the fact that such operations are a constant possibility and feel "at the mercy" of such an attacker. However, in this case, the risk of escalation is extraordinarily high. This will briefly be addressed below.

Fifth, as a special case, a doctrine of "Digital Media Control" could demonstrate a capability to orchestrate cyber information operations. The strategic impact of such operations can be significant. An example is the late appearance of the anti-muslim hate video of Coptic Christian extremists in the USA, causing widespread chaos and anti-west hostilities in the Middle-East. This counts as a special case of cyber operations, however, as these operations do not necessarily require hacking capabilities. They rather consist of a combination of conventional capabilities to spin information operations and the knowledge of how to place these effectively in digital media. Yet such capabilities could be counted into the realm of cyber operations, and their mastery could have a significant deterrent effect under specific circumstances.

As a special case of the doctrine of "Digital Media Control", o doctrine of "Attribution Control" could evolve over time. If a state demonstrates a mastery of attribution as an ability to make others believe a certain kind of attribution, he shows that he is capable of orchestrating false-flag operations. This can have a deterrent effect in itself. A defender would have to fear that the deterring party would always be capable to escalate existing tensions between the defender and a third party.

It is noteworthy that all these kinds of deterrent uses of cyber capabilities do not have a linear, in-kind deterrent effect on foreign cyber operations. These can always take place anyhow—as the attacker cannot be identified. In-kind deterrence will not be an aim of cybered deterrence. It will rather simply add a new tool to the conventional apparatus of deterrence, but in specific ways as specific scenarios can be suggested by the kinds of capabilities demonstrated.

Force Posture of Cybered Deterrence

How would the forces necessary for cybered deterrence be demonstrated? This will not work along the lines of conventional deterrence. Cybered deterrence does not establish itself by the number of cyber weapons on the shelf. It rather consists of the quality of the military hackers. So force posture will have to be a proof of an intellectual potential. This can be undertaken by means of a single impressive cyber weapon, field-tested in the wild or within controlled conditions. But it's more likely going to consist of a number of different measures. As a first step, an actor will have to prove his potential by soft measures. He will have to demonstrate efforts and investments in research and development, in personnel or agencies. But more specif- ically—as he has to prove mastery of those assets, not just possession—an actor will have to launch a series of different, sophisticated cyber attacks onto different targets.

Most of these attacks will be plain, sub-conflict access attacks. From a tech- nical point of view, it is completely possible to spread such "unarmed" cyber attacks. These attacks simply penetrate high-security systems and sit there with- out doing anything apart from occupying space for as long as possible, thus demonstrating the weakness of the defender. But more serious kinds of demonstra- tions are possible as well. A system difficult and complex to attack, with a reli- able amount of resilience, could be targeted and switched off for a short period of time. This would cause only minor damage. But it would demonstrate extreme mastery of cyber warfare. A synchronized short blackout in a small number of non-networked, heterogenous critical infrastructures would be an example. Such an attack would be extremely difficult in preparation, design and operation, thus demonstrating very high capabilities, if successful. If not successful, attacks like these can be dangerous. If the blackout turns constant, complex catastrophes could evolve, especially if the attacker chose to additionally switch off the mechanisms of safety engineering, providing emergency procedures and backup plans.

Another important feature for force postures can be adopted from the hacking community. This community is very competitive, and judges the quality of hacks mainly by their "elegance". Elegance is demonstrated either by causing something previously deemed impossible, by causing something complex with a very few simple, novel moves, or by causing something simple and exotic in a very com- plex machine. The more the moves used for this are entirely novel and innovative, the more modules and stages of the attack are elegant in design and operation, and the less code is needed, the better. This kind of quality assessment can be directly transferred to cybered deterrence. A group of military hackers demonstrating a high degree of elegance in their hacking in a number of either strictly controlled armed or less-controlled unarmed attacks will always be more deterring than less elegant hackers. Elegance will also be assessed in other things. An example is the automation of an attack. Most attacks on high-security systems have limited options for feedback mechanisms. So the attacks have to be automatized to a certain degree, maybe even as "fire-and-forget". This is an extremely demanding specification, especially in complex, secret systems with a lot of safety and security engineering embedded. If such a task can be mastered, mastery is demonstrated quite well.

Cybered Deterrence Dilemmas

Two dilemmatic effects can be mentioned, following from cyber deterrence postures. First, a demonstrated ability to engage in cyberwarfare in an atmosphere dominated by the problem of attribution will automatically render any actor who demonstrated cyber capabilities into a potential cause of future cyberincidents. In other words: if one has demonstrated to be able to undertake a certain kind of hacking, and something like that happens without any clear identification, he will automatically be among the suspects. For some actors with less resilience or tolerance towards such accusations, this might cause a kind of self-deterrence not to use the tools demonstrated lightly. In order to avoid escalation, once one has demonstrated mastery of this new kind of weaponry, one has to behave more responsibly. But this only holds of course as long as the overall number of players is not too large—an evolutionary stage we will soon leave.

Cyber deterrence might also cause another, more substantial dilemma. If many state actors have demonstrated mastery of offensive cyber capabilities, including mastery of anonymity, then states in defense, whose economies and other assets are under constant attack by unknown attackers and with largely unknowable consequences (as it is the case now), might tend to interpret this kind of "business as usual" with all its uncertainties as part of a strategy of erosion led against them by their preferred adversary. In fact, judging from a perspective of responsible statecraft, states might even be well advised to assume the worst. The damage could be very high. They would have to react appropriately. But since the attacker is not legally identifiable and since no single one of the smaller incidents per se will justify harsh reactions, it is unlikely that a conventional conflict will be started over this kind of activity. Something else is more likely. States might feel justified to quietly compensate their potential losses to maintain their strategic status. To achieve this in proportion, the easiest way would be an in-kind compensatory "hackback". Such defenders would pick up offensive hacking themselves, in the very way they receive it, and steal and spy and manipulate themselves. This, however, would only lead to more attacks and more uncertainty about their strategic impact, thus causing others to engage in precautious compensatory hackbacks as well, which will also reinforce the attempts of the initial attackers so they can keep up. A "compensatory hackback spiral" towards massive offensive, state-led hacking could evolve which might eventually cause a real-world escalation as well.[2]

A Comparison of Cybered Deterrence and Nuclear Deterrence

Classical nuclear deterrence is summarized by the so-called "Mutual Assured Destruction (MAD)" doctrine. A more thorough analysis shows that, in order to get the premises of a MAD posture, you need, among others:

- an invulnerable second-strike capability by nuclear actors;
- definite "professional" nuclear (civilian and military) organizations, so that the "nuclear key" is in the hands of credible actors that are resistant to deterrence failures or deliberate (or accidental) nuclear wars;
- the possibility to regulate the nuclear arena through specific nuclear strategic disarmament treaties with definite verification/monitoring mechanisms;
- the establishment, during the Cold War, of a nuclear logic banning the ballistic missile defense systems (the famous ABM Treaty in the 1972–2002 period) so that to reduce the risks of the temptation of decapitating first-strikes;
- a capability to inflict "unacceptable damages" to another country.

Using cyber threats as a deterrent force doesn't fit these characteristics in a number of aspects:

- The malleability of attribution and the potentiality of multipolarity of cyber attacks pose difficulties for the framing of a classical deterrence doctrine. These difficulties could be overcome by an agreement on formal communication to enable formal attribution.
- Other differences can be noted as, in cyberspace, a possibility of multiple-strike capabilities by any kind of actor exist, and as the retaliatory capabilities do not necessary fit an action-reaction scheme, and can rest for long times.
- Cyber attacks can be launched not only by "professional organizations". Indeed any criminal organization, non-state actors and "groups-of-power" could do that, even if cyber malwares like "Stuxnet", "Flame", etc. should require high-professional organizations, multidisciplinary skills and very expensive costs (however extremely low compared to the one endorsed by, for instance, keeping nuclear forces operative and on high alerts).

---

[2] To address a popular question in this respect: an arms race situation in a quantitative sense is not systemically inherent. A certain number of sophisticated military hacking capabilities could be considered sufficient without a need to buy more. The only arms race which could develop from cyber deterrence would be a race to cover all kinds of abilities. But this would rather have to be regarded as a conventional arms races in cyber.

- The bottom line here is that the "human dimensions" of potential cyberwarfare and their "professional organizations" are extremely difficult to gauge, assess and "balance".
- More important is the complete absence of any international framework or convention or treaty to restrain cyberwarfare (like the famous strategic nuclear treaties of the Cold War). Furthermore, cyberwarfare, due to its much less indirect nature, doesn't raise the taboo associated with the nuclear mushroom in public opinions and in political arenas. In fact, at least to date, it is hard to only sufficiently sensitize publics and policy makers for the threat at all.
- Cyber defense can be built at several layers and for different sensitive targets and in principle, all countries that are capable of cyberattacks have the possibility to raise cyber defenses (as well as to pursue cyberwarfare capabilities). Therefore, under this token, a cyberwar can be won (a nuclear war cannot), and a "Cyber Assured Destruction (CAD)" can be avoided or at least mitigated by establishing different levels of defenses and creating impenetrable communication information networks against any external, but also internal, malicious efforts. Such a variant of high security information technology does not exist right now, and developing and implementing it might be far away from the present, due to technical and monetary challenges, but it is not impossible to the same degree as nuclear defenses.
- Last, but not least, it is difficult to imagine equally "unacceptable damages" (geographically and over time) in the case of a cyberwar. Military cyber attacks might be capable to cause substantial and strategically highly important losses or disruptions, but again, this will not be to the same extent as if caused by nuclear weaponry.

The conclusion of this preliminary comparative analysis between nuclear deterrence and cyberdeterrence seems to hint that cyberwarfare has not the same deterrent value as nuclear deterrence. However, it carries a potential to construct new deterrent postures as mentioned above. These postures could be used as an addendum by nuclear powers for more precise and sub-conflict deterrence in post-cold-war environment, but also, more importantly, by other political powers to enable a certain level of strategic deterrence against high-tech nations. This lends additional weight to the ongoing efforts of the UN to search for an international (not legally-binding) "Code-of Conduct (CoC)" for cybersecurity. In case of the EU, a separate CoC could be pursued as a matter of a specific initiative by the competent Directorate General of the EC.

Potential Actors and the Right Narrative

Who will choose to make use of cybered deterrence? The more established powers are probably less of a concern. They will add cybered deterrence to their overall deterrence posture. But they are equally vulnerable, and due to their other deterrent capabilities, less likely to risk conflicts. So these actors might not tend to use cybered deterrence a lot—even though it offers some elegant options. In this context, one could also imagine that, for these global players, "cyber deterrence deters only cyber weapons".

Some of the non-established powers are more likely to engage more frequently in this kind of warfare. Cyber warfare and cybered deterrence in particular offer a lot of benefits for them. There are risks too, of course. Foreign intelligence services might identify and annihilate them, or they might not be able to define the thresholds in the right way. But some nations could decide that these risks are manageable for them. Opportunities create interests. Cybered deterrence might find some takers.

However, one has to be very careful which kinds of capabilities to demonstrate if one wants to engage in cybered deterrence. Cybered deterrence postures should be designed as strategic narratives, as specific stories being told to the world or— if their activities can be well contained—to a specific adversary. Such narratives should also take into account certain failures, and how to compensate those. And they should be aware that a demonstration of cyberpower might make them an easy target of accusations and probably cyber-retaliations in the future, whether those are warranted or not.

Cyber deterrence can be a very powerful addendum, and a flexible and mighty tool in international relations. But is also entails a number of risks to be accounted for. Any state choosing to engage in this kind of game should enter it with great awareness and care.

Cybersecurity and Cyber Weapons: Is Nonproliferation Possible?

Clay Wilson

Abstract *"Cybersecurity and Cyber Weapons: is Nonproliferation possible?"* by Clay Wilson, deals with the argument that several international organizations now describe malicious codes as a Weapons of Mass Destruction (WMD), and argue that nations are entering a new cyber arms race. Dr. Wilson questions whether it is possible to manage the global spread of malicious cyber weapons by using methods for nonproliferation in the ways they were used to control traditional nuclear weapons. The paper also discusses emerging threats from malicious cyber code, and describes characteristics of cyber weapons that some organizations now classify as Weapons of Mass Destruction, similar to Chemical, Biological, Radiological, or Nuclear (CBRN) WMD.

Introduction

Iran has recently seen its ongoing nuclear program disrupted by malicious cyber code that damaged hundreds of delicate centrifuges used for uranium enrichment. China and Russia are suspected of stealing huge amounts of sensitive economic data, and possibly secret military data from U.S. computers. These events have occurred because cyberspace offers a rapid and inexpensive way to use malicious code as tools or weapons to exploit significant but subtle weaknesses in computers and software. These weapons can enable espionage to shift the balance of economic or military power, or to secretly control and damage critical infrastructure equipment, possibly leading to large-scale loss of essential services. In an essay in the Wall Street Journal July 19 2012, President Barack Obama warned that "the cyber threat to our nation is one of the most serious economic and national security challenges

C. Wilson (✉)
IWG and University of Maryland University College, Adelphy, MD, USA
e-mail: clay.wilson@umuc.edu

M. Martellini (ed.), *Cyber Security*, SpringerBriefs in Computer Science,
DOI: 10.1007/978-3-319-02279-6_2, © The Author(s) 2013

we face." National Security Agency director Keith Alexander reportedly said that cyber espionage constitutes "the greatest transfer of wealth in history".

Several international organizations now describe malicious code as a Weapon of Mass Destruction (WMD), and argue that nations are entering a new cyber arms race. The characteristics that place malicious code into this new WMD category include stealthy code used for cyber espionage that can exflitrate state-secret data, or code that can enable destruction of critical infrastructure property.

Nonproliferation agreements have been used in the past to reduce the spread of nuclear arms, and may be needed again to help keep cyber weapons out of the hands of extremist groups, and possibly lower tensions between nations. This article questions whether it is possible to manage the global spread of malicious cyber weapons by using methods for nonproliferation in the ways they were used to control traditional nuclear weapons. The unique qualities of malicious cyber code may reduce or defeat the effectiveness of past methods for managing nonproliferation.

This article discusses emerging threats from malicious cyber code, and describes characteristics of cyber weapons that some organizations now classify as Weapons of Mass Destruction, similar to Chemical, Biological, Radiological, or Nuclear (CBRN) WMD. The global market for purchase of malicious cyber code is described, in addition to the researchers who create the zero-day exploits that help enable the operation of cyber weapons. The conclusion presents several questions that must be considered by policy makers before it is possible to effectively manage nonproliferation of cyber weapons.

Critical Infrastructure Facilities are Now Targets

Recently, it was revealed that cyberattacks targeted against Iran's top secret nuclear facilities. Flame and Stuxnet were identified as two examples of malicious code that were used to conduct cyber espionage against Iran, and also destroy critical laboratory equipment. The Flame espionage code was inserted into the networks of many Middle East countries, where it remained undetected for a considerable period of time. It remained undetected in Iran's classified network for nuclear enrichment possibly for several years, quietly mapping the network, activating cameras and microphones of internal office PCs, and transmitting large amounts of state-secret information back to a central source. Stuxnet code was inserted into networks around the globe, but it was designed to become active only in the networks of Iran's top secret nuclear facility. Once it determined that it was into the targeted system, it operated to cause specific critical industrial equipment to self-destruct, while at the same time displaying false readings on the safety system gauges monitored by Iranian technicians. Some observers believe that Flame and Stuxnet may have been cyber weapons that were designed to work together to target and destroy Iran's nuclear facility. Flame may have mapped Iran's secret network to lay plans for the damage done later by Stuxnet. Sources in 2012 estimate the damage from Stuxnet may have set the Iranian nuclear program back by 18 months or more.

Invasive and Destructive Cyber Weapons Resemble Nuclear WMD

After observing how Flame and Stuxnet may have worked together to delay the Iranian nuclear program, some organizations now describe malicious cyber weapons as WMD. Code that can infiltrate classified systems to map and transmit date, and also destroy critical infrastructures have been placed into this category. In a recent article, The Bulletin of Atomic Scientists observes that the new development of cyber weaponry actually parallels the past development and use of nuclear weapons:

> Consider the similarities: First, government and scientific leaders invent a new kind of weapon out of fear that others will develop it first and threaten the United States. Second, the consequences of using the new weapon—both the material damage it might cause as well as its effects on international security and arms-race dynamics—are poorly understood. Third, scientists and engineers warn political and military leaders about the dangers of the new weapon and call for international cooperation to create rules of the road. Fourth, despite warnings by experts, the US government continues to develop this new class of weaponry, ultimately unleashing it without warning and without public discussion of its implications for peace and security.

U.S. Acknowledges Development of Cyber Weapons

While current rules of engagement restrict the military from taking actions outside of its own computer networks without special permission, the United States government recently acknowledged being involved in the development of cyber weapons, starting in 2006 with a classified program named "Olympic Games". Many observers suspect the US and Israel may have worked together to develop the highly successful cyberattacks against Iran. However, although U.S. officials have acknowledged involvement with the development of Stuxnet, as of this the U.S. has not openly acknowledged deploying cyber weapons against another country.

In August 2012, the U.S. Air Force, in a public procurement document, announced that it was requesting concept papers for building offensive cyber weapons with capabilities for cyber warfare attack, to destroy, degrade, deceive, and corrupt targeted computer systems. Also in August 2012, the Air Force Research Laboratory reportedly gave six firms Indefinite Delivery-Indefinite Quantity (IDIQ) contracts valued at up to $300 million under a program called Agile Cyber Technologies (ACT). These firms reportedly are tasked to remain on standby to provide cyber weapons on-demand. The cyber weapons may be designed to defend Air Force networks, spy on enemy networks, or conduct offensive cyber attacks.

In 2012, DARPA announced a $110 million research program named Project X, reportedly intended to give U.S. military commanders the capability to target and disable specified computer systems anywhere on the Internet. The research also seeks to create pre-planned attack and counter-attack scenarios that do not involve human intervention before they are launched.

U.S. military officials are also reportedly researching cyber weapons that can target "offline" military systems in part by harnessing emerging technology that uses radio signals to insert computer coding into networks remotely. This portends development of a new generation of cyber weapons capable of disrupting enemy military networks even when those networks are not connected to the Internet.

Characteristics of Cyber Weapons

A zero-day exploit is malicious cyber code designed to take advantage of a vulnerability that is newly-discovered and as yet unknown to computer operators and software vendors. Zero-day exploits are used within cyber weapons to gain a stealth capability, to defeat or bypass security and gain entry into otherwise secure computers. Because the vulnerabilities are newly-discovered, there is no defense against a zero-day exploit. This can only change after the presence of the cyber weapon has been discovered through careful observation, or sometimes accidental detection of unusual computer activity by systems and network administrators. Then, effective countermeasures can be created to block the cyber weapon, but usually only after the unique attack methods of the enabling ZDE have been analyzed. The subtle and unusual characteristics of a ZDE are what prevent traditional anti-virus software and other cyber defenses from detecting them. Sometimes, months or years can pass until a systems administrator may notice some unusual operation or suspicious transmission occurring in an infected computer system.

> Using data from the computers of 11 million users who opted into security firm Symantec's antivirus telemetry and reputation services, two researchers looked for any malware that exploited vulnerabilities before the security issues had been publicly disclosed. Sifting through the large data set, they found 18 zero-day attacks, including 11 attacks that the industry had not previously discovered. The attacks lasted anywhere from 19 days to 30 months, with an average lifetime of 312 days before public disclosure of the vulnerability...

Once a security countermeasure is developed and distributed, the zero-day exploit can be blocked. However, a quiet zero-day exploit retains a high value for the user until after it is discovered by the target. Meanwhile, the cyber weapon can quietly steal sensitive data, monitor keystrokes, activate audio and video systems to spy on users, or prepare targeted equipment for carefully-timed destruction.

Iran Creates its Own Cyber Command

In response to Stuxnet, Iran reportedly has now created its own new Cyber Command. Brig. Gen. Gholamreza Jalali, the head of Iran's Passive Defense Organization, reportedly said that the Iranian military was now prepared "to fight our enemies" in "cyberspace and Internet warfare," a formula that may imply aspirations to go on the offensive. Other observers have predicted this evolution to creation of new cyber commands, as nations move to protect their national security in cyberspace. In addition, larger states with deeper vulnerabilities and larger budgets will anticipate and actively disrupt attackers, as well as defend against the attacks that are thrown against them. This evolution into offense was anticipated because future cyberattacks may spread too fast, or become too difficult to detect before an effective defense can be implemented. Future national security in cyberspace may require each country to create a cyber command that combines defense, preemptive cyberattacks, and cyber espionage. This is the existing model for the U.S. Cyber Command.

Reports Link Iran to Cyberattacks Against U.S. and Allies

Heightened international tensions over Iran's progress with its nuclear program may be leading to reports with attribution errors. Senator Joseph Lieberman has stated that Iran is suspected to have launched cyberattacks that were intended to disrupt computers in U.S. banks, including JP Morgan Chase and Bank of America. Officials also blamed Iran for possibly launching cyberattacks against Aramco oil in Saudia Arabia and other Middle East countries that are cooperating in an oil embargo against Iran. These latest destroyed data on hard drives, shutting down several Aramco oil company systems for several weeks. However, recent reports by investigators indicate the cyberattack against Aramco may not have been launched by Iran after all, but rather the work of a lone hacker who inserted a flash-drive into a PC behind the company firewall. Errors in the design of the malicious code and other aspects of the virus, dubbed Shamoon by researchers, offered evidence that the attack in Saudi Arabia most likely was perpetrated by a single individual. Investigators reportedly stated that part of the Shamoon virus was taken from an off-the-shelf product made by Eldos Corporation, a London-based security company. However, whether or not attribution to Iran is accurate, the increasing number of reports about cyberattacks that damage equipment can add fuel to concerns about development of a possible cyber arms race.

New Cyber Arms Race

The cyberattacks directing Stuxnet against critical infrastructure in Iran could also be viewed by some as an act of cyber warfare. It can be said that through deployment of the Stuxnet malicious code, the U.S. and Israel may have helped energize a new cyber arms race. And now, copies of both of these advanced cyber weapons are in the hands of many nation-states and sophisticated hackers.

Michael Rake of BT Group PLC reportedly warned that world powers are being drawn into a high-tech arms race, with many already able to fight a war without firing a single shot. "I don't think personally it's an exaggeration to say now that basically you can bring a state to its knees without any military action whatsoever," Rake said. He said it was "critical to try to move toward some sort of cyber technology nonproliferation treaty."

International Tensions Have Created New Market Forces

There is now a growing market where organizations purchase zero-day exploits to use for espionage, theft of intellectual property, or possible disruption of equipment. Researchers around the world now find they can offer malicious code for sale to governments, to industries, or to other organizations to help gain competitive advantage, or to prepare the groundwork for future economic or cyber warfare. Prices are going up and this has incentivized many highly-skilled cyber researchers into becoming more mercenary.

The zero-day tools are now bought and sold as part of an expanding global market which is not illegal in some countries. The brokers and middlemen now operate fully-structured businesses, and the buyers and sellers for each transaction are kept anonymous. The sale price is not revealed, and of course the purpose for each zero-day exploit is kept secret.

The recent Stuxnet and Flame cyberattacks may have boosted demand in the global market for buying and selling of cyber weapons for espionage or destruction. Highly-skilled independent technical researchers now have discovered that sophisticated cyber weapons can be sold in a secretive global market for huge sums. Customers include nation states and businesses, and the cyber weapons in demand are those that have exploits that can remain on infected computers for months or years before they are detected, all the time conducting espionage for a central source, or possibly awaiting commands to damage equipment. Brokers now operate legitimate, if questionable, businesses to sell these zero-day exploits to customers globally, and perhaps also to extremist groups or their proxies.

However, when a new set of malicious code is released into the Internet, it can eventually be detected, copied, reengineered by researchers, and then sold to attack other targets by the new owner. Every cyber weapon contains its own blueprint which can then be used to make a newer cyber weapon. The cyber espionage capability demonstrated by Flame, and the destructive cyberattack by Stuxnet could also work equally well against factories, the electric grid, or other critical infrastructure operations that are inside the U.S. or other Western countries. The threat from these types of malicious code is now considered a national security issue.

Despite requiring the buyer to sign a contract that restricts any resale, it is not possible for a broker to control whether a malware product won't be sold again to another organization. The concern is that some day, if not already done, one of the malicious zero-day exploits will be sold by a middleman to an extremist organization and used to attack the critical infrastructure of the U.S. or another country. However, other observers feel that, because of the large amounts of data being stolen through cyber espionage, reportedly by China, the Western countries may fall behind in economic and political power. Therefore, they must purchase or create their own zero-day exploits to monitor and prevent cyberattacks against industries.

The Growing Problem for Internet Security

When organizations purchase cyber weapons with zero-day exploits, they potentially drive up the global market prices. This makes entry even more attractive to highly-skilled researchers and middlemen. One possible outcome may be an increase in the price to all organizations for maintaining strong cybersecurity. This may lock in a process that assures the internet will become less and less secure for all other users.

While a government or other organization is using a zero-day exploit, they must also keep a secret about the existence of the vulnerability that is being attacked. While keeping the secret, it means the country's own national infrastructure may remain vulnerable to a similar cyberattack. Therefore, countries that are engaged in a secret arms race may be deliberately leaving their own populations and critical infrastructures open to unnecessary risk.

As effective as Stuxnet and Flame are reported to be, cyber weapons are now only at the beginning stages of development. After Stuxnet had been detected by Iran and removed from its nuclear facility systems, according to a report by the IAEA, the country was able to boost output enough to reverse all Stuxnet-induced production losses and achieve a new level of uranium enrichment that exceeded the pre-Stuxnet trend. However, in the future we are likely to encounter cyber weapons that have capabilities beyond Flame or Stuxnet—cyber weapons that cannot be deleted, or weapons that can be transmitted wirelessly to infect computers.

Concerns About Nonproliferation

A major concern of global organizations such as the International Atomic Energy Agency (IAEA) is exploring ways to reduce the proliferation of weapons of mass destruction. WMD has traditionally comprised Chemical, Biological, Radiological, and Nuclear (CBRN). In the age of Cyber and Information Technologies, the IAEA and other international organizations have expanded discussions of nonproliferation to include management of cyber weapons. The acronym "CBRNCy" (Chemical, Biological, Radiological, Nuclear, and Cyber) is now used by the International Working Group, Landau Network Centro Volta, to include new cyber threats as part of their ongoing discussions of WMD and nonproliferation.

In 2012, China and the U.S. met to discuss concerns about the increasing threat to national security from development of cyber weapons. Systems in China have been linked to cyber espionage against U.S. military and business computers. However, after stories emerged about the effects of Stuxnet on the Iranian nuclear program, China reportedly sees itself as increasingly vulnerable to cyberattacks from the U.S. Although China, along with Russia, reportedly supports doctrine, such as the International Code of Conduct for Information Security, the U.S. is not in agreement. The reason is that such a treaty would likely include restrictions on free speech, which could possibly violate the U.S. Constitution.

Some security experts, including Eugene Kaspersky, the researcher whose laboratory discovered the existence of Stuxnet, reportedly feel that cyber weapons should be banned by international treaty. Observers are divided about the wisdom of a cybersecurity treaty. Francis Delon, France's secretary-general for national defense and security, reportedly stated that it was too early for work toward an international pact because policymakers were still coming to grips with the ways that states—and criminals—could strike at each other over the Internet. As for some kind of cyberweapon nonproliferation treaty, Delon seemed dismissive. However, others have suggested that the International Telecommunication Union could act as a kind of online version of the International Atomic Energy Agency, which polices member states' nuclear programs with inspections and monitoring.

> Both Russia and the United States agree that cyberspace is an emerging battleground. Russia favors an international treaty along the lines of those negotiated for chemical weapons and has pushed for that approach at a series of meetings this year and in public statements by a high-ranking official. Russia's proposed treaty would ban a country from secretly embedding malicious codes or circuitry that could be later activated from afar in the event of war....However, the United States argues that a treaty is unnecessary. It instead advocates improved cooperation among international law enforcement groups. If these groups cooperate to make cyberspace more secure against criminal intrusions, their work will also make cyberspace more secure against military campaigns, American officials say. But American officials are particularly resistant to agreements that would allow governments to censor the Internet, saying they would provide cover for totalitarian regimes. These officials also worry that a treaty would be ineffective because it can be almost impossible to determine if an Internet attack originated from a government, a hacker loyal to that government, or a rogue acting independently. The United States is trying to improve cybersecurity by building relationships among international law enforcement agencies...

Barriers to Nonproliferation of Cyber Weapons

The oversight and verification mechanisms in the Strategic Arms Reduction Treaty (START) gives the U.S. insight into what the Russians were doing with their nuclear weapons, but it relies upon positive verification measures. However, malicious cyber code could possibly remain undetected until after thousands of computers globally had been secretly infected and later activated to attack, thus avoiding verification efforts completely.

Managing nonproliferation for cyber weapons may require methods that differ from assuring nonproliferation of traditional CBRN weapons. Detection of a cyber weapon during development may be difficult or impossible. Monitoring to spot advance preparations of malicious cyber weapons may itself require the use of cyber espionage tools, an act that expands the use of malicious code.

Protection, resilience, and preemptive strike are common themes for nonproliferation, but cyber threats are anonymous, inexpensive, and undetectable in advance. Restrictions may remain unverifiable. Preparation and seeding of malicious code to lay the foundation for a larger cyber threat may take place over several years prior to activating a coordinated cyber weapons attack. Traditional methods for managing the spread of CBRN weapons of mass destruction may not work for cyber weapons.

International tensions are heightened when one government or group is thought to be stealing state-level secrets or large amounts of economic information from other countries, or thought to be possibly mapping internal systems for a future cyberattack. Attribution is still difficult, so governments can carry out deceptive cyberattacks to which they cannot be linked. As a result, many countries may now use their own zero-day exploits to monitor activities of other governments for self-defense, or to monitor activities of extremist groups.

Unique Characteristics of Cyber Weapons

Cyber weapons may prove to be absolutely undetectable. Zero-day exploits can be developed on a private network not connected to the Internet. They can be quietly deployed through the Internet, and secretly embedded in many targeted computer systems. An anonymous controller may send a signal to direct infected computers to transmit secret intellectual property back to a central collection point, or at a carefully-chosen moment, possibly direct computers to shut off valves that might cause an explosion at a sensitive industrial facility.

Stuxnet and Flame were both effective as cyber weapons because they contained zero-day exploits that allowed them to operate while remaining undetected for long periods of time. Stuxnet may have contained at least four zero-day-exploits. The code for Flame is reported to be at least 20 times larger and much more sophisticated than Stuxnet. As security procedures are gradually increased for computer facilities, the level of sophistication found in newer zero-day exploits will continue to elevate, along with the level of skills needed by the developer.

The Growing Market for Malicious Code

Many code builders have very secretive associations that are spread across international boundaries, and their privacy is protected by encrypted communications and exclusive membership based on referral and reputation as a superior coder. Individuals with the skills necessary to create sophisticated, malicious code are often actively recruited by a variety of organizations, including law enforcement agencies, and cash-heavy criminal organizations. The appeal to join may be generated either through a sense of patriotism, or for money, or to support extreme political views.

Researchers can demand between $5,000 and $250,000 for a single zero-day product. Sales of zero-day exploits include an exclusive license to a single customer, and the targeted software product vendor is not alerted. Payments to the middleman can be made in installments.

For a long time, researchers and hackers were content to trade zero-day exploits only with each other, mainly for prestige. Brokers and middlemen have developed fully-structured businesses to handle all details to connect researchers with buyers. Brokers reportedly now receive between 12 and 14 zero-day exploits from researchers every month, an increase of almost triple the number of zero-day exploits that were created for sale just a few years ago.

Today the market for zero-day exploits is secretive and unregulated, and the current environment encourages the creation and sale of cyber weapon exploits around the world. Sales can be made through the Internet to criminal organizations, who may then offer to rent their technical services to others to deploy malicious code against a target. Extremist groups, some with ties to criminal organizations, may possibly be able to put forward proxies to participate with brokers in the sale or rental of services.

> An example of a middleman company is Vupen, based in France, which has advertised a malware product for sale that can break into the Google Chrome browser. They have refused to reveal the nature of the vulnerability to Google and have instead offered to product for sale to "customers". Vupen has stated that its customers are limited to national security agencies of several NATO countries for purposes of lawful intercept of communications, and to protect democracy. However, the list of Vupen customer countries reportedly also includes Belarus, Azerbaijan, Ukraine, and Russia.

Netragard is another example of a broker company which buys exploits from researchers and then reportedly only sells them to companies inside the U.S.

Buyers of cyber weapons may someday include extremist groups. Currently, many sales are reportedly made to the U.S. government, European agencies, and supporting contractors, such as Northrop–Grumman and Raytheon. Government agencies often explain to the providers that they intend to use the malware to monitor communications of criminal suspects, or disable the computers and phones of suspects and targets for intelligence gathering. The customers who represent Western governments reportedly pay the highest market prices for malicious exploits. Market prices are kept low in Russia, where there is reportedly too much criminal activity which interferes with business transactions, and in China where there is reportedly a large population of internal hackers and researchers who sell only to the government of China. Markets in the Middle East reportedly cannot yet match the higher prices offered by Western governments. However, most technology has a way of reducing its cost as time progresses.

> The governments who buy zero-day exploits also bear responsibility here. The U.S. administration has repeatedly warned of a crippling cyber-attack to our infrastructure, and

Congress is in the midst of debating an expansive new "cybersecurity" bill that, as EFF previously explained, will likely invade users' privacy in the name of promoting Internet security. Yet the sale and use of exploits that leave ordinary users of popular software vulnerable—a real cybersecurity threat—remains unmentioned in this cybersecurity debate.

Export Restrictions Under ITAR and Wassenaar

It is not clear if current regulations will help with nonproliferation of zero-day exploit code. In the past, vendors of cyber encryption tools had to register as an arms dealer and obtain an arms license from the State Department. Encryption was on the U.S. Munitions List and export was regulated by the International Traffic in Arms Regulations (ITAR). Under ITAR, any article or service on the United States Munitions List (USML) requires an export license issued by the United States State Department. However, "software" has been treated as expression under copyright law, and the U.S. Supreme Court holds that the First Amendment prohibits the government from restricting the languages used by its citizens.

The Wassenaar Arrangement on Export Controls for Conventional Arms and Dual-Use Goods and Technologies requires transparency on deliveries of equipment which can be used for both peaceful and military aims. It is not clear what exact requirements must be met for zero-day exploits to be legally classified as military.

Questions to Consider for Cyber Nonproliferation

1. Can existing policies to manage nonproliferation of traditional CBRN also work for cyber weapons? Nuclear non-proliferation worked because many of the technologies and raw materials were specialized and traceable. Nonproliferation of malicious zero-day cyber tools is difficult to enforce because the production and distribution may be undetectable.
2. Is cyber espionage essential for national self-defense? Cyber espionage has contributed to theft of state secrets and other economic intellectual property, which has heightened international tensions.
3. How can highly-skilled, and highly-paid researchers become engaged to help restrict the spread of zero-day exploits and cyber weapons?
4. Should zero-day exploits be subject to export controls? What will be required to legally classify zero-day exploits as military weapons?
5. Should any policy related to cyber security ensure that vulnerabilities are fixed, and explicitly disallow any clandestine operations within governments that do not further this goal?
6. Should regulations require transparency for all sales transactions involving zero-day exploits?

Conclusion

Critical infrastructure systems are now targets for cyberattacks as evidenced by the use of Flame for cyber espionage inside Iranian nuclear facilities, and use of Stuxnet to destroy uranium enrichment equipment. As a result, some international organizations now describe cyber weapons as WMD. The U.S., Iran, and other countries are now actively seeking to enhance their own capability to use cyber weapons. International tensions have helped fuel a secretive market for sale of cyber weapons built by groups of entrepreneur researchers to buyers that may include governments, businesses, and perhaps extremist groups. Experts fear that nations are entering a new cyber arms race that parallels the development and use of nuclear weapons.

These trends have greatly reduced overall cyber security for all users of the Internet. Past methods for assuring nonproliferation of WMD have relied on tracking and inspections of materials required for constructing CBRN weapons. However, the unique characteristics of cyber weapons remove the need to gather special materials for development, and the incorporation of zero-day exploits enables them to be deployed for future cyberattacks in ways that are undetectable.

The characteristics of cyber weapons indicate that past methods to manage the spread of traditional CBRN will likely not be successful for reducing the proliferation of cyber weapons. The international community will need to discuss these issues to create policy that effectively controls the spread of cyber weapons.

Bibliography

D. Alexander, After early successes, Obama struggles to implement disarmament vision. Chicago Tribune (2012). http://articles.chicagotribune.com/2012-08-31/news/sns-rt-us-usa-nuclear-armsbre87u06b-20120830_1_nuclear-weapons-new-start-treaty-world-without-nuclear-arms. Accessed 2 Sept 2012

J. Ball, Regulations eyed for cybersecurity trade. Washington Post (2012). 2 Sept 2012, p. A6

K. Benedict, Stuxnet and the bomb. Bulletin of the Atomic Scientists (2012). http://www.thebulletin.org/web-edition/columnists/kennette-benedict/stuxnet-and-the-bomb. Accessed 20 Sept 2012

R. Carroll, US urged to recruit master hackers to wage cyber war on America's foes. The Guardian (2012). http://www.guardian.co.uk/technology/2012/jul/10/us-master-hackers-al-qaida?newsfeed=true. Accessed 22 Aug 2012

P. D. Demchak, *Rise of a cybered westphalian age* (Air University Strategic Studies Quarterly, Spring, 2011), pp. 32–61

P. Dodds, Web summit considers cyber-nonproliferation pact. ECN News (2011). http://www.ecnmag.com/news/2011/06/web-summit-considers-cyber-nonproliferation-pact. Accessed 2 Sept 2012

M. R. Engleman, Code in aramco cyber attack indicates lone perpetrator. Bloomberg (2012).http://www.bloomberg.com/news/2012-10-25/code-in-aramco-cyber-attack-indicates-lone-perpetrator.html. Accessed 29 Oct 2012

Solicitation Number FA8750-12-R-0002, FedBizOps.gov. Agile Cyber Technology (ACT) (2011). https://www.fbo.gov/index?s=opportunity&mode=form&tab=core&id=15674b71f7e098c64710ff953a567ba4&_cview=0. Accessed 28 Oct 2013

A. B. Greenberg, Meet the hackers who sell spies the tools to crack your PC [and get Paid Six-figure Fees]. Forbes (2012a). http://www.forbes.com/sites/andygreenberg/2012/03/21/meet-the-hackers-who-sell-spies-the-tools-to-crack-your-pc-and-get-paid-six-figure-fees/. Accessed 3 Sept 2012

A. B. Greenberg, Shopping For zero-days: a price list for hackers' secret software exploits. Forbes (2012b). http://www.forbes.com/sites/andygreenberg/2012/03/23/shopping-for-zero-days-an-price-list-for-hackers-secret-software-exploits/. Accessed 3 Sept 2012

J. Griffin, Flame: a cyber weapon of mass destruction. TMCnet.com. (2012) http://www.tmcnet.com/topics/articles/2012/05/29/292267-flame-cyber-weapon-mass-destruction.htm. Accessed 20 Sept 2012

N. Hoover, Air force seeks offensive cyber weapons. Information Week (2012). http://www.informationweek.com/air-force-seeks-offensive-cyber-weapons/240006574. Accessed 20 Sept 2012

S. Kemp, Cyberweapons: Bold steps in a digital darkness?. Bulletin of the Atomic Scientists (2012). http://www.thebulletin.org/web-edition/op-eds/cyberweapons-bold-steps-digital-darkness. Accessed 20 Sept 2012

J. M. Kramer, US and Russia differ on treaty for cyberspace. New York Times (2009). http://www.nytimes.com/2009/06/28/world/28cyber.html?_r=1&pagewanted=all. Accessed 2 Sept 2012

R. Lemos, U.S., china talks address cyber-weapons, not cyber-spying. eWeek (2012). http://www.eweek.com/c/a/Security/US-China-Talks-Address-CyberWeapons-not-CyberSpying-329861/. Accessed 20 Sept 2012

R. Lemos, Zero-Day attacks long-lived, presage mass exploitation. Dark Reading – Techweb (2012). http://www.darkreading.com/advanced-threats/167901091/security/attacks-breaches/240009358/zero-day-attacks-long-lived-presage-mass-exploitation.html?cid=nl_DR_daily_2012-10-19_html&elq=64756851392a414db40239930e4e457d. Accessed 19 Oct 2012

C. Miller, The legitimate vulnerability market: the secretive world of 0-day exploit sales. Independent Security Evaluators (2007). http://securityevaluators.com/files/papers/0daymarket.pdf. Accessed 3 Sept 2012

Ministry of Foreign Affairs of the Peoples Republic of China:. China, Russia and Other Countries Submit the Document of International Code of Conduct for Information Security to the United Nations (2011). http://www.fmprc.gov.cn/eng/wjdt/wshd/t858978.html. Accessed 15 Sep 2012

E. Nakashima, With Plan X, pentagon seeks to spread U.S. military might to cyberspace. Washington Post (2012a). http://www.washingtonpost.com/world/national-security/with-plan-x-pentagon-seeks-to-spread-us-military-might-to-cyberspace/2012/05/30/gJQAEca71U_story.html. Accessed 4 Sept 2012

E. Nakashima, U.S. accelerating cyberweapon research. The Washington Post (2012b). http://www.washingtonpost.com/world/national-security/us-accelerating-cyberweapon-research/2012/03/13/gIQAMRGVLS_story.html. Accessed 29 Oct 2012

R. Naraine, 0-day exploit middlemen are cowboys, ticking bomb. ZDNet.(2012). http://www.zdnet.com/blog/security/0-day-exploit-middlemen-are-cowboys-ticking-bomb/10294. Accessed 3 Sept 2012

P. Paganini, Reflections on the zero-day exploits market. Infosec Island (2012). http://www.infosecisland.com/blogview/20819-Reflections-on-the-Zero-Day-Exploits-Market.html. Accessed 3 Sept 2012

N. Perlroth, In cyberattack on saudi firm, U.S. sees iran firing back. The New York Times (2012). http://www.nytimes.com/2012/10/24/business/global/cyberattack-on-saudi-oil-firm-disquiets-us.html?pagewanted=all. Accessed 20 Apr 2013

J. Reed, Coming soon on demand: cyber weapons. Foreign Policy: National Security (2012). http://killerapps.foreignpolicy.com/posts/2012/09/05/coming_soon_on_demand_cyber_weapons. Accessed 30 Oct 2013

Daily Maily Reporter, Weapons of cyber mass destruction: U.S. and Israel behind Stuxnet worm attack on Iran, expert claims. Mail Online (2011). http://www.dailymail.co.uk/news/article-1362847/Weapons-cyber-mass-destruction-U-S-Israel-Stuxnet-worm-attack-Iran-expert-claims.html. Accessed 20 Sept 2012

D. Sanger, Obama order sped up wave of cyberattacks against Iran. The New York Times (2012). http://www.nytimes.com/2012/06/01/world/middleeast/obama-ordered-wave-of-cyberat-tacks-against-iran.html?pagewanted=all&_moc.semityn.www. Accessed 20 Sept 2012

N. Shachtman, Russia's top cyber sleuth foils US spies, helps kremlin pals. Wired (2012). http://www.wired.com/dangerroom/2012/07/ff_kaspersky/all/. Accessed 10 Sept 2012

M. H. Timm, Zero-day exploit sales should be key point in cybersecurity debate. Electronic Frontier Foundation (2012). https://www.eff.org/deeplinks/2012/03/zero-day-exploit-sales-should-be-key-point-cybersecurity-debate. Accessed 3 Sept 2012

C. Wilson, Science collaboration and security: emerging cbrncy challenges and threat reduction programs beyond 2012 (Presentation at the International Working Group, Landau Network Centro Volta Workshop - Evolving, Existing and New Threats Stemming from Cyber and Information Technology Sectors, Como, Italy, 2012)

Cyber Security for Nuclear Power Plants

Thomas Shea, Sandro Gaycken and Maurizio Martellini

Abstract *Cyber Security for Nuclear Power Plants* by Thomas Shea and Sandro Gaycken and Maurizio Martellini is a meticulous analysis of the current situation regarding the security of Nuclear Power Plants. It describes the current stage, outlining the motivations of potential cyberattacks and how they could be carried out. It proceeds in presenting an all-comprehensive security circle that provides opportunities for engagement and collaboration to deal with cyberissues at various levels. Since this paper was presented at the Seoul Nuclear Security Summit of 2012, it ends with useful recommended action for the Summit to take, in order to ensure that the peaceful use of nuclear energy is not vulnerable to cyberattacks.

Setting the Stage

Nuclear power plants may be vulnerable to cyber attacks, which might—in extreme cases—lead to substantial releases of radioactive material with consequent loss of lives, radiation sickness and psycho-trauma, extensive property destruction and economic upheaval.

Today's cyber attacks are made on computer systems operated for a wide spectrum of purposes. Until now, no cyber attacks on nuclear power plants have resulted in releases of radioactive material, but the trends are disquieting. The

T. Shea (✉)
IWG and TomSheaNuclear Consulting Services, West Richland, WA, USA
e-mail: tomsheanuclear@me.com

S. Gaycken
IWG and Freie Universitat Berlin, Berlin, Germany
e-mail: s.gaycken@fu-berlin.de

M. Martellini
IWG and Landau Network – Centro Volta, Como, Italy
e-mail: maurizio.martellini@centrovolta.it

M. Martellini (ed.), *Cyber Security*, SpringerBriefs in Computer Science,
DOI: 10.1007/978-3-319-02279-6_3, © The Author(s) 2013

objective of a cyber attack may not be to cause death and destruction, for example, but to disrupt the operation of a nuclear facility, to inflict economic damage, to embarrass government or utility officials, to blackmail companies, to get even, or just to test one's skills or to see what happens. There is even a risk of cyber attacks aimed at other targets migrating into nuclear facilities and causing unpredictable damages. The overly large distribution of Stuxnet has demonstrated this possibility. Given the potential for great harm, any successful cyber attack on a nuclear facility would—at the least—undermine confidence in the ability of the State to be a responsible host and the owner and operator to run the facility in a safe and secure manner.

Cyber attacks may be intended to have local and limited effects, but radioactive material ejected from a failed reactor pays no heed to national boundaries.

Foreign governments, groups hostile to the government of a given State, or individuals motivated by greed, hatred or curiosity may carry out Cyber attacks. The systems intended to deter and defeat such threats must address all potential perpetrators, taking into the consideration the range of motivations noted above:

a. Cyber attacks carried out by the citizens of a state against targets within that state may violate the laws of the state intended to protect the public health and welfare and may be identified as acts of domestic terrorism;
b. Cyber attacks created by activities outside the targeted state or affecting other states in addition to the targeted state may be considered as acts of international terrorism[1];
c. Cyber attacks carried out by or under the aegis of foreign governments may be considered as acts of war[2];
d. Cyber attacks in certain circumstances might be classified as crimes against humanity.

Contemporary nuclear power plants rely extensively on a large and diverse array of computers for a host of tasks. Some computers may play a role in monitoring or controlling the operation of the reactor itself or of ancillary systems. The nuclear power plant operating and technical support staff commonly uses computer networks, and connections may exist between these systems and plant control systems, sometimes known, sometimes not known. If the hard- or software used is modified or replaced, the reactor might be forced into an accident and the emergency response systems may fail to prevent calamity.

In principle, a plant employee acting alone might accomplish such an attack either acting on his/her own volition or under duress. Or, fabricated hardware or

---

[1] The International Convention for the Suppression of Acts of Nuclear Terrorism states in Article 2.1 that "Any person commits an offence within the meaning of this Convention if that person unlawfully and intentionally: (b) Uses in any way radioactive material or a device, or uses or damages a nuclear facility in a manner which releases or risks the release of radioactive matter."

[2] "The Pentagon has concluded that computer sabotage coming from another country can constitute an act of war, a finding that for the first time opens the door for the U.S. to respond using traditional military force."

software introduced into the plant might contain surreptitious instructions that might be activated according to preset conditions, once in use.[3] Or, an attempt may be made to hack into the protective systems making it possible to take over the plant controls externally, from within the plant, within the State or virtually anywhere in the world.

Some such scenarios are known and have even been tested:

- In one case, a group of hackers successfully manipulated the displays in the operating center, forcing the employees into false and potentially catastrophic reactions.
- In another case, hackers were able to gain control of the cooling system of a nuclear power plant.

Hacking in general and attacks on "protected" computer systems are becoming increasingly common and more sophisticated. All of these concerns above demand robust proactive countermeasures to prevent successful cyber attacks—the cost of inadequate protection may be disastrous. While reported nuclear cyber attacks events are rare no so far not cataclysmic, the threat trajectory suggests that ignoring cyber security may place individual nuclear power plants at risk, some more seriously than others.

Moreover, in addition to the direct consequences of a successful attack, the axiom that 'an accident in any nuclear power plant is an accident in all nuclear power plants', would likely extend to a security event—including a cyber attack. A successful cyber attack on a nuclear reactor with substantial consequences would undermine global public confidence in the viability of nuclear power.

Some states are apparently establishing the ability to engage in such attacks, probing defensive barriers, exercising tests of cyber weapons or simply protecting their security by creating the ability to engage in cyber warfare in case the need arises.

Cyber security in relation to nuclear facilities is under increasing scrutiny. It is described in many publications, nowhere more cogently than in a "backgrounder" note provided by the US Nuclear Regulatory Commission.

The 2012 Nuclear Security Summit in Seoul will take up the issue of cyber security. The Summit should address the key underlying questions in order to establish a future course of actions. How real is the threat? How and when should it be addressed? What mechanisms already exist for the international community to combat this global menace? What else is needed? What should the Summit agree to, and what steps should be taken collectively following the Summit—directly, as part of the Security Summit process, and indirectly, by States, international organizations and other bodies?

---

[3] In such circumstances, the cyber attack may have been unforeseen and unintended, but the originator of the worm or virus may still be prosecuted on the basis of the end results. Nuclear operators must ensure that casual vulnerabilities are blocked; no security system should contain unintended holes.

Domains for Engagement

The extent to which a nuclear power plant is vulnerable to such attacks will depend upon the design of the plant,[4] the technical and organizational history of the plant, how and which computers are used, whether the computers allow for internal and/or external networked interactions, and how effective the counter-measures employed are at preventing such attacks or mitigating the consequences of any attacks that succeed.

Some problems can best be dealt with nationally while others have to be dealt with internationally. National approaches can mobilize national technological and legal assets, giving less cause for dispute. International efforts should be driven by three concerns: firstly, the fact that a threat against a state may originate in a foreign land and the impact could affect other States; secondly, that a threat to one State today may presage an attack on another tomorrow; and thirdly, that international investment may help to strengthen the resolve of the international community and may provide more robust and secure hard- and software.

While nuclear cyber threats are in many ways unique, the security environment reflects interests common to other concerns. The security cycle presented below provides opportunities for engagement and collaboration at various levels.

1. *Threat definition*: Each State and each nuclear utility must assess the potential for cyber attacks that could result in major consequences. Specific models for threat assessment have to be developed to achieve this kind of oversight. Anticipating cyber threats from past events has not proven to be a viable method. Cyber threat modeling must include the types of malicious actors in question, their differing capacities for cyber attacks, the costs and benefits of attacks, typical and individual vulnerabilities providing potential attack vectors and) the security profile for the State, including the extent to which adversaries threaten the State, and the extent to which cyber attacks occur. Cyber threat modeling should quantify and rank the threats and identify appropriate countermeasures. (The IAEA offers assistance to States seeking to develop a design basis threat to serve as the basis for all protective measures, and its mission could be expanded along these lines.)
2. *Legal infrastructure*:
    a. The international community needs to review regularly whether the treaties and other measures in place are adequate. Such measures should reflect the fact that a cyber attack on a nuclear power plant with the intention of substantial radiation releases should be considered as act of terrorism and hence be prohibited by the International Convention for the

---

[4] On December 26, 2011, the United States Nuclear Regulatory Commission gave the green light to Westinghouse's 1,100 MWe AP1000 pressurized water reactor design. The NRC said the design incorporates passive safety features that would cool down the reactor after an accident without the need for human intervention. The design provides enhanced safety margins through use of simplified, inherent, passive, or other innovative safety and security functions.

Suppression of Acts of Nuclear Terrorism or a crime against humanity subject to other relevant anti-terrorism treaties, the Convention on the Physical Protection of Nuclear Material, the Nuclear Safety Convention.

b. It is incumbent on the national government of each State to establish an inter-departmental response to the threat of cyber attacks on nuclear power plants, including its national security structure in all of its dimensions. It may be appropriate to define such arrangements within an existing governmental body or to create a new agency for this and related purposes.

c. It is further incumbent on each national government to enact legislation together with subordinate regulations and guidelines consistent with its legal structure and the threats it faces, in conformance with its treaty obligations and other considerations.

3. *Intelligence*: It is essential for a State to continually search for information on States, organizations and individuals who might engage in cyber attacks, and to devise appropriate response mechanisms. While protecting sensitive sources, each government should keep all nuclear utilities informed of emerging threat information. Nuclear utilities in turn have to be able to comprehend threat information and assess their individual potential impact.

4. *Capability development*: Each State must determine its national requirements and seek to establish national programs to detect, block and determine the source of hacking attacks. If detection is unlikely to be effective, security concepts have to be developed which compensate the loss of capabilities of early warning and crisis management. Capability development also includes educating experts to specialize in cyber security. (Standardized educational certifications to signify sufficient expertise are necessary and need to be created.) Cooperation with trusted States or international organizations could significantly enhance the cost-effectiveness of national and utility programs.

5. *Cyber security systems implementation*: At the level of each reactor, the utility should implement a robust system aimed at reducing potential vulnerabilities and preventing cyber attacks. Such a system should include the following elements:
   a. A detailed IT mapping of each nuclear facility;
   b. Limiting network access, preferably disconnecting all critical areas from networks;
   c. Highly hardened information security with standards to be determined by international bodies;
   d. Capabilities for detecting abnormal instructions;
   e. Capabilities for detecting attempts to gain access or to escalate access privileges;
   f. Provisions and procedures for informing the national command authority;
   g. Provisions and procedures for engaging law enforcement, as appropriate; and
   h. Provisions and procedures for informing international bodies, as agreed by the national government.

Table 1 The International Nonproliferation Regime is the sum of its authorities, actors and activities

Authorities	Actors	Activities
National Laws and Regulations	Public (or parts thereof)	Create nonproliferation culture diminishing appeal of nuclear weapons
UN Charter, esp. Chapter VII	Sovereign National Governments and Agencies	Encourage states to accept binding nonproliferation commitments
UN Security Council Resolutions (including 1540)	Regional Control Bodies (EURATOM, ABACC)	Promote proliferation-resistant nuclear technology and commercial arrangements
Proliferation Security Initiative Agreed Principles	United Nations and UN Security Council	Obtain intelligence and other information on a state's nuclear activities
Treaty for the Nonproliferation of Nuclear Weapons (the NPT)	International Atomic Energy Agency (IAEA)	Verify design information, absence of diversion or clandestine production of nuclear material, weaponization
IAEA Statute	Nuclear Suppliers Group and Zangger Committee	Investigative reporting, scholarly analysis
IAEA Safeguards Agreements	Nuclear Vendors	Deny suspicious export requests and notify appropriate states & organizations
Nuclear Suppliers Group and Zangger Committee	Nuclear Facility Operators	Interdict illicit trafficking in nuclear materials
Nuclear Supply Commercial Contracts	Non-governmental Organizations (e.g., World Institute of Nuclear Security, World Nuclear Association)	Use diplomacy to address suspected acts of noncompliance
Nuclear Facility Policies, Procedures and Practices	Professional Societies (e.g., Institute of Nuclear Materials Management, European Safeguards Research & Development Association)	Apply sanctions to compel compliance
Nuclear Weapon Free-Zone Treaties	National Laboratories and Universities	Employ military force as a last resort
Comprehensive Test Ban Treaty (not in force)	Armed Forces	
Fissile Material Cutoff Treaty (negotiations not underway)		

Readers are advised to use the table as three separate lists. More than one of the elements in one column will influence or be affected by more than one element in the other columns. The table is useful for determine interrelationships and steps to be considered when addressing specific situations

6. *Law enforcement*: Depending on the circumstances of individual attacks, the site security force, local law enforcement, national law enforcement and

international bodies, especially Interpol, should be prepared to respond and be engaged as soon as possible. Law enforcement agencies have to develop sufficient capacities in the field of IT-forensics, including the undeveloped field of IT-forensics of Industrial Control Systems (ICS).

7. *System assurance*: What steps should be taken at each level from a specific nuclear power plant up to the international community to guarantee that adequate protection is in place. Controls should be implemented to monitor compliance. Liabilities for non-compliance should be formulated. In addition, methodologies and certificates have to be given out to distinguish insufficient security technologies and configurations from effective ones.

8. *Lessons learned*: Characteristics of each attempt should be analyzed to determine the need for system modifications. Reviews of cyber attempts should be broadened to include the national government and all nuclear utilities, neighboring States (excluding adversaries), and the international community. To ensure cooperation, protocols for trusted information sharing have to be created and obligations to disclose such information have to be formulated.

Nuclear Terrorism and the Proliferation of Nuclear Weapons

Concerned with the threats associated with the proliferation of nuclear weapons, over the years the international community has created a remarkable non-proliferation regime. It is imperfect, as all things human are, but it is extensive and represents something unique in international relations. It is and likely will always remain a work in progress, evolving to meet new challenges and implementing new capabilities. Its elements are shown in Table 1. Its extent and pervasiveness reflect the all nations except for the remaining few interested in acquiring nuclear arsenals support the regime and continue to join in additional steps to make it perfect.

It may be appropriate now to create a parallel table describing the national and international measures undertaken in relation to the prevention of nuclear terrorism, including cyber-terrorism, even if the likelihood of cyber terrorism is very low at present.

Cyber attacks may be directed at military or civilian targets including virtually any computer used for any purpose. Nuclear power plants or fuel cycle facilities could be attacked by other means involving force or guile; attacks by military forces are not within the scope of the Summit, however, attacks aimed at taking over or destroying nuclear power reactors carried out by para-military forces clearly is and on that basis, nuclear cyber attacks should be addressed.

Recommended Actions for the Seoul Nuclear Security Summit

Taking into account the potentially extreme consequences of a cyber attack on a nuclear reactor (especially) or on a nuclear fuel cycle facility, recognizing that nuclear facilities may already be reasonably well protected against credible threats today, and acknowledging that the trajectory of threats is a matter of uncomfortable speculation, we believe that the Seoul Nuclear Security Summit should take prudent steps to ensure that the peaceful use of nuclear energy is not vulnerable to cyber attack and that the international efforts directed as a result of this consideration are chosen so as to build strength and trust among States embarking on prudent and legitimate peaceful uses of nuclear energy. We recommend the following specific steps.

Definitions

The Summit should seek to define terms related to this topic, including nuclear cyber threat, nuclear cyber attack and nuclear cyber security according to the potential for damage, the motivation and the outcome; e.g., as presented above. The definitions should include the full range of possible attacks, ranging from those made by clever individuals to attacks mounted by or on behalf of a hostile government or terrorist organization.

a. Cyber attacks carried out by the citizens of a State against targets within that State may violate the laws of the State intended to protect the public health and welfare and may be identified as acts of domestic terrorism;
b. Cyber attacks created by activities outside the targeted State or affecting other States in addition to the targeted State may be considered as acts of international terrorism;
c. Cyber attacks carried out by or under the aegis of foreign governments may be considered as acts of war; or
d. Cyber attacks may be considered as crimes against humanity.

Legal Authority

The Summit should create the legal frameworks necessary to ensure that States protect themselves against domestic and international nuclear cyber attacks:

a. Each State should enact and enforce legislation to prevent cyber attacks on nuclear reactors and nuclear fuel cycle facilities, detect and apprehend perpetrators and punish individuals or organizations operating within the territory of a State responsible for or abetting such activities.

b. States should examine the provisions of existing conventions (especially the Convention for the Suppression of Acts of Nuclear Terrorism and the Convention for the Physical Protection of Nuclear Material) with the intention of identifying interpretations and/or modifications as necessary to extend their provisions to include domestic and international nuclear cyber-terrorism.

c. Using once again its extraordinary authority under Chapter VII of the Charter of the United Nations, the Security Council should determine whether existing Resolutions 1373 and 1540 should be amended to address nuclear cyber terrorism, and whether under specific circumstances acts of nuclear cyber terror should be identified as crimes against humanity.

d. The Summit should examine the role of specific regional and international organizations in relation to the prevention, detection and resolution of nuclear cyber attacks, to seek a clear and streamlined ability to confront the threats of nuclear cyber-terror, including Interpol, the International Telecommunications Union (ITU), the UN Group on Information Security, the International Atomic Energy Agency, EURATOM and ABACC.

Protective Measures

The Summit should organize and oversee investigations into technical and administrative barriers that would prevent cyber attacks from succeeding.

Capability

The Summit should:

a. Define the specific human skills required to protect against nuclear cyber-terrorism, and create internationally recognized standards and certifications to confirm that the people involved are adequately prepared for their work[5];

b. Identify education and training institutes engaged in this field and encourage cross fertilization;

c. Encourage the development and presentation of "best practices" in cyber security[6];

d. Encourage further work by professional societies and national bodies to create standards affecting cyber security;

---

[5] The World Institute of Nuclear Security (WINS) might undertake such activities.

[6] Such activities are already underway by the IAEA and WINS.

e. Encourage continued R&D into protection against cyber attacks on nuclear reactors and nuclear fuel cycle facilities;
f. Define computer hardware and software intended to be immune to cyber attacks;
g. Using probabilistic risk assessments identifying failure modes for nuclear reactors and nuclear fuel cycle facilities, define methods and procedures for facility officials and national security officials to test the adequacy of applied counter-cyber terrorism systems;
h. Define mechanisms for detecting the source of cyber attacks;
i. Establish communication arrangements and associated security protocols to facilitate information sharing and problem solving; and
j. Remain seized of the issue and the importance of prevention.

Creation & Sharing of Relevant National & International Intelligence

The Summit should encourage States to share intelligence on evolving threats and information associated with the source of any attack.

Cyber Security Systems Implementation

The Summit should explore alternative means through which States seeking assurance in the cyber security systems they employ could provide advice, recommendations on system hardware, software, expert advice, quality assurance and certification, including performance requirements for facility-level systems, national systems, and the response capabilities suitable for local law enforcement.

Law Enforcement

The Summit should provide encouragement and possibly funding as needed to assist States concerned about their ability to protect against nuclear cyber attacks. The Summit should ensure that essential international bodies receive cooperation and financial support as necessary to excel in performing their required functions.

Lessons Learned

The Summit should create a mechanism for reviewing progress in relation to the prevention of nuclear cyber terrorism, including progress by States, advancement of counter-cyber terrorism measures, and systematic a posteriori reviews of attacks that have occurred—including those that fail and those that succeed.

Bibliography

G. Cauley, Hearing on Discussion Draft Legislation to Improve Cybersecurity of the Electric Grid NERC (2011), http://www.nerc.com/news/testimony/Testimony%20and%20 Speeches/HECC%20May%2031%20Cauley%20Testimony%20Final.pdf Accessed 4 Mar 2013

S. Gorman, J. Barnes Cyber Combat: Act of War. WSJ (2011), http://online.wsj.com/article/SB1 0001424052702304563104576355623135782718.html. Accessed 4 Mar 2013

IAEA Development, Use and Maintenance of the Design Basis Threat, IAEA Nuclear Security Series (2009), http://www.pub.iaea.org/MTCD/publications/PDF/Pub1386_web.pdf. Accessed 4 Mar 2013

United Nations Yearbook of the United Nations (1989), http://books.google.com/ books?id=MLAxV20gktQC&pg=PA294&lpg=PA294&dq=prevention+of+military+at tacks+on+nuclear+reactors&source=bl&ots=E1dBq3-VC-&sig=XfjvTxy1I92E7HuNb 4pgE1Bibcg&hl=en&sa=X&ei=gKIIT8G1BYa0iQLcqvyZCQ&sqi=2&ved=0CD4Q6A EwBQ#v=onepage&q=prevention%20of%20military%20attacks%20on%20nuclear%20 reactors&f=false. Accessed 4 Mar 2013

Interpol Cybercrime (2012), http://www.interpol.int/Crime-areas/Cybercrime/Cybercrime. Accessed 4 Mar 2013

G. Keizer, Is Stuxnet the 'best' malware ever?. ComputerWorld (2010), http://www. computerworld.com/s/article/9185919/Is_Stuxnet_the_best_malware_ever_. Accessed 4 Mar 2013

B. Kesler, The Vulnerability of Nuclear Facilities to Cyber Attack. Strategic Insights **10**(1), 15−25 (2010).

LCG Consulting NRC Approves Rule to Amend AP1000 Nuclear Reactor Design (2011), http://www.energyonline.com/Industry/News.aspx?NewsID=7552&NRC_Approves_Rule_ to_Amend_AP1000_Nuclear_Reactor_Design. Accessed 4 Mar 2013

The International Electrotechnical Commission. Standards addressing cyber security: http://www.iec.ch/dyn/www/f?p=103:30:0::::FSP_ORG_ID,FSP_LANG_ID:1358,25. (Accessed 4 Mar 2013), especially Standard 45A/846/CD, IEC 62645 Ed.1: Nuclear power plants - Instrumentation and control systems - Requirements for security programmes for computer-based systems

The World Institute of Nuclear Security. Workshop on the security of Information Technology (IT) & Instrumentation and Control (IC) Systems at Nuclear Facilities, February 27–29, in Ontario, Canada (2012). See: http://www.wins.org/. Accessed 4 Mar 2013

United Nations (1999–2002), The rome statute of the international criminal court. http://untreaty. un.org/cod/icc/statute/romefra.htm. Accessed 4 Mar 2013

United Nations (2001), UNSCR 1373 http://www.un.org/News/Press/docs/2001/sc7158.doc.htm. Accessed 4 Mar 2013

United Nations (2005) ,International convention for the suppression of acts of nuclear terrorism. http://www.un.org/en/sc/ctc/docs/conventions/Conv13.pdf. Accessed 4 Mar 2013

Cyber Security for Chemical Plants

Maurizio Martellini, Stephanie Meulenbelt and Krzysztof Paturej

Abstract *"Cyber Security for Chemical Plants"* by Maurizio Martellini, Stephanie Meulenbelt and Krzysztof Paturej provides a technical analysis of possible cyber attacks towards critical infrastructures in chemical industry and chemical safety. The paper analyses attacks and possible countermeasures such as those aimed at sabotage, those exploit the SCADA systems like Stuxnet, and those aimed at espionage, such as Flame. The paper also pictures a possible involvement of the Organization for the Prohibition of Chemical Weapons (OPCW) in cyber security for chemical plants.

Introduction

Security officials have always concentrated on physical protection to prevent critical infrastructure from intrusions, but systems inside facilities are (often) linked to computers and controlled via networks and cyberspace. This has left industrial control systems vulnerable to attack.[1] The number of cyber incidents and the sophistication of the attacks have dramatically increased and cyber-attacks

---

M. Martellini (✉)
IWG and Landau Network-Centro Volta, Como, Italy
e-mail: maurizio.martellini@centrovolta.it

S. Meulenbelt
TNO, Delft, The Netherlands
e-mail: stephanie.meulenbelt@tno.nl

K. Paturej
IWG and Ministry of Foreign Affairs, Warsaw, Poland
e-mail: krzysztof.paturej@msz.gov.pl

---

[1] Industrial control systems are computerized systems that open and close valves, switches, and factory processes vital to the chemical, industrial, and power sectors.

M. Martellini (ed.), *Cyber Security*, SpringerBriefs in Computer Science,
DOI: 10.1007/978-3-319-02279-6_4, © The Author(s) 2013

increasingly target critical infrastructure, including chemical plants.[2] A cyber-attack on a chemical facility could be perpetrated for different reasons, including espionage to monitor progress made or steal information. It could also be used as a means to disrupt the operation of a facility. This could lead to (substantial) releases of (toxic) chemicals and may cause loss of lives, injuries, property destruction and/or economic damages. In order to ensure the safety of workers, the public, and the environment, it is of utmost importance to (continue to) advance the protection mechanisms of chemical plants' computer networks to reduce vulnerability to cyber-attacks.

The potential consequences of hacking into a plant's control station via computers and digital devices had been made evident by a 2007 experiment called the "Aurora Project", performed by the Idaho National Laboratory in the US. By rewriting the Industrial Control System (ICS) computer code for the power generator, attackers caused it to shake and produce smoke. The vibrations disabled the machine and caused (permanent) damage. Ultimately, the experimenters were able to direct it to self-destruct. This project did not only demonstrate that plants' information systems can be penetrated and controlled by cyber commands, but also that cyber commands alone can destroy industrial equipment. The Idaho National Laboratory, in cooperation with the United States' Department of Homeland Security, also exhibited a cyber-attack on a mock-up of a chemical facility. In the exercise, a small group of attackers staged an assault on the chemical plant, using concepts that are relevant in the real world, such as: exploiting corporate trust; subverting a system's security by (spear) phishing, for instance, by sending an e-mail to a company representative that appears to be from a friend or a legitimate business partner, but which contains malicious software and can open a link between the sender's computer and the corporate computer; and 'the man in the middle', that is, sending out false sensor signals to trick the system and its operator into thinking that the equipment is running as usual, while in fact a virus is taking over control of (certain) plant activities.

Possibilities of online intrusions on industrial control systems are thus not theoretical. The discovery of the so-called 'Stuxnet worm' in June 2010, which is believed to be the first worm designed to target real-world critical infrastructure, including industrial units, made clear that an actual threat exists. The worm was particularly significant as stealing and/or manipulating data or financial reward[3] was not its purpose. Rather, it intended to take over control by manipulating industrial control systems to operate outside their intended instructions. It was a (cyber) weapon meant to achieve a kinetic effect and designed to target a particular type of industrial control system; Programme Logic Controllers (PLCs) made by engineering multinational Siemens. It intended to gain access to Supervisory Control

---

[2] In 2011, the US Industrial Control Systems Cyber Emergency Response Team (ICS-CERT) received 198 reports of incidents, compared to just nine incidents reports in 2009.

[3] The virus was infecting Microsoft's Windows operating systems using several flaws that had not been detected before (called a "zero days"). Such flaws can be sold on the black market for as much as $100,000 each.

And Data Acquisition (SCADA) systems, which are industrial control systems for monitoring and managing industrial infrastructure or facility-based processes.[4]

Stuxnet moved from computer to computer, attempting to spread to every machine on that computer's network and to find out whether any were running particular software. If not, Stuxnet left the system alone. If so, the worm checked to see whether the machine is connected to a PLC or waits until it is. It then finger-prints the PLC and the physical components connected to the controller, looking for a specific kind of machinery. When it found what it was looking for, it injected its own rogue code into the controller, to change the way the machinery works. During the sabotage of the targeted system, the virus fooled the machine's digital safety system into reading as if everything were normal; it recorded what normal operation looks like and then played back those readings to the plant operators.

After extensive research, experts agree that the particular piece of machinery Stuxnet was looking for was hardware used for uranium enrichment activities in the Iranian Natanz nuclear site. The virus was calibrated to spin out of control the centrifuges at that facility. Stuxnet hunted down PLCs that are running motors at high speed, because they are more likely to be controlling centrifuges. It is not publicly known what damage the virus caused exactly; Iranian authorities claim that no or limited harm has been done, but other sources put forward that the attacks resulted in the paralysis of a substantial part of the power plant's computer networks, causing a delay in Iran's nuclear programme. One still speculates about the damage the virus could have inflicted if it had been discovered at a later point in time, or not at all.

In 2011, another virus, called "Duqu", was discovered. As some parts of it were nearly identical to Stuxnet, experts think that it was written by the same authors, or at least by people having access to the Stuxnet source code.[5] In contrast to Stuxnet, Duqu does not intent to sabotage any industrial process. Nevertheless, its discovery has reignited fears about cyber-attacks targeting systems behind equip-ment at critical infrastructure such as power plants, water treatment facilities, and chemical plants. It is believed that Duqu intends to gather intelligence data and assets such as blueprints or design documents that could help attackers to mount a future attack on various industries.[6] It targets entities such as industrial infrastruc-ture and system manufacturers, but works highly selective; only a limited number of suppliers to industrial facilities have been infected for their specific assets. Six organisations in eight countries have been targeted for sure—companies in France,

---

[4] SCADA systems are used to monitor and control processes in industrial facilities and public utilities, such as chemical plants, electric power plants, refineries, oil and gas pipelines, wastewa-ter treatment, and other installations. Large and complex SCADA installations can cover a large geographical area, especially if they include a grid.

[5] The recovered samples have been created after the last-discovered version of Stuxnet.

[6] For Stuxnet to be effective, for instance, its creators needed to know exactly the computer con-figurations that were used in the facility in Natanz. Traces of an early version of Stuxnet, explor-ing, scanning, and recording what it found, have been found in 2009. It is believed that the Duqu virus serves a similar purpose.

the Netherlands, Switzerland, the Ukraine, India, Iran, Sudan, and Vietnam—but it is highly likely that other entities have become a victim of the virus as well.

One of the latest cyber threats discovered is the "Flame(r)" virus, which was identified by computer experts in mid-April 2012. Flame appears to infect computers disguised as legitimate Microsoft Windows update and is considered the most complex virus discovered so far. Once a system is infected, Flame begins a complex set of operations, including sniffing the network traffic, taking screenshots of on-screen activity, intercepting the keyboard, automatically detecting when certain programs such as email or chat are open, and so on. It can change computer settings, remove data off hard drives, activate audio systems to listen in on Skype calls or office chatter or even steal data from Bluetooth-enabled mobile phones. Furthermore, attackers created the possibility to put in additional modules to perform specific tasks in a similar way as adding apps to a Smartphone. Flame has been detected across the Middle East; in the Palestinian territories, Sudan, Syria, Lebanon, Saudi Arabia, and Egypt, but the virus has struck Iran the hardest, where it penetrated the oil sector among others.[7] It is believed that by the time the virus had been contained, computers and websites from the National Iranian Oil Company, the National Gas Company, the Ministry of Oil and several subsidiary companies had already taken a hit. Several oil terminals were disconnected from the Internet as a precautionary measure, and a crisis committee was formed to deal with the fallout and strengthen defences.

Identifying the Threat

For developing viruses like Stuxnet, Duqu, and Flame, substantial financial and technological resources as well as manpower were needed. However, now that the codes are "in the open", the viruses could be analysed and repurposed for future attacks. This means that anyone with a computer has the potential to inflict harm. If one knows its way around specific features of particular controllers and has a good understanding of how operations in their target facilities are designed, one could perpetrate very precise attacks, damaging only the designated targets. However, an attack on a chemical facility, for instance, could lead to the release of chemical substances and large surrounding areas, much larger than the target area, could be contaminated. Furthermore, the scenario where people without relevant expertise launch attacks exists as well. The smallest mistake in the development of a self-replicating virus could lead to an uncontrollable virus that escapes the intended targets, infecting computers all over the world. Cyber security experts are concerned about industry not being hardened enough against attacks. Many

---

[7] The Iranian oil sector was at the time already struggling to combat another virus called "Wiper". The Wiper virus has erased data on hard drives inside the Iranian Ministry of Oil in April 2012. Wiper could be one of Flame's command modules.

companies in the chemical areas, for instance, focus almost 100 % on physical security and have done little or nothing (yet) with cyber security. Experts warn that access to a company's corporate system can allow hackers to penetrate the vital industrial control processes, manipulate pressure and other control system settings, potentially leading to explosions or other dangerous conditions. Thus, as long as improved security systems have not been developed, chemical industry is running a risk. It seems particularly vulnerable to cyber espionage and sabotage.

Cyber Espionage

Cyber espionage includes covertly capturing electronic communications such as e-mail traffic and text messages, corporate data that is valuable from a commercial point of view or for the purpose of gathering national-security intelligence. It can involve the theft of industrial technology and state secrets. For instance, in February 2011, hackers were found to have conducted a multi-year cyber espionage campaign directed at global oil, energy, and petrochemical companies; the "Night Dragon attacks". The attackers leveraged command and control servers on purchased hosted services and compromised servers to conduct attacks to acquire proprietary and highly confidential information. Perpetrators used social engineering, spear-phishing attacks, hacking tools that exploited Microsoft operating systems, and remote administration tools to copy and extract information. They successfully took highly sensitive, competitive information, including proprietary information about oil- and gas field operations, project financing and bidding documents. The virus focused on the energy sector, but the tools and techniques of this kind of attack can be highly successful when targeting any industry.

Another cyber-attack session, one that appears to have been designed to target chemical firms, and primarily private companies involved in the research, development, and manufacturing of chemicals and advanced materials, is "Nitro".[8] The attacks began in late July 2011 and lasted until mid-September of that same year. The goal of the attackers appeared to be collecting intellectual property, including formulas, and design and manufacturing processes. The attackers send emails to employees of selected organisations, asking them to open an attachment, claiming to be meeting invitations from established business partners or necessary security updates. The attachments contained a 'self-extracting executable' containing

---

[8] A total of 29 companies in the chemical sector were confirmed to be targeted in this attack wave and another 19 in various other sectors, primarily the defence sector, were seen to be affected as well. These 48 companies are the minimum number of companies targeted and likely other companies were also targeted. Companies affected include: Multiple Fortune 100 companies involved in research and development of chemical compounds and advanced materials; Companies that develop advanced materials primarily for military vehicles; and companies involved in developing manufacturing infrastructure for the chemical and advanced materials industry.

PoisonIvy, a common "backdoor Trojan" developed by a Chinese speaker.[9] When attempting to open the attachment, users would unknowingly install PoisonIvy, which would contact a server using an encrypted communication protocol, enabling attackers to issue instructions to the compromised computers and search for higher-level passwords to gain access to servers hosting confidential information. Generally, once they identified the desired intellectual property, attackers would copy the content to archives on internal systems they use as internal staging servers. To complete the attack, the content was then uploaded to a remote site outside of the compromised organisation. This way, attackers were able to widely spread the virus. Chemical companies in Bangladesh, the UK, and, primarily, the US held the majority of infected computers. One of the leading US chemical enterprises, Dow Chemicals, for instance, confirmed that it had been one of the targets of "unusual emails", but engaged internal and external response teams, including law enforcement, to address the situation. They believe that their adequate action prevented operations of being compromised.

Sabotage

Viruses like Night Dragon, Duqu, and Nitro include persistent attempts to steal valuable information, mainly focusing on stealing intellectual property such as SCADA operations data, design documents, and other information that could cause business harm. That pattern of espionage should raise fresh alarms in the corporate world about information theft, as this information could be used to make a competitive or counterfeit products, out-bid a rival for an exploration lease, coordinate a marketing campaign against a competitor's new product, and so on. Not only is this a problematic development in a (free) market economy, as it could frustrate competition between rivalling companies, also, there is a possibility that intelligence gathered by these viruses will be used for mounting future attacks on industrial facilities.

In the world of chemical processing, where efficiency is critical, an undetected cyber attack can slow the computer's response, the network's speed or frustrate an entire process, reducing the efficiency, or even destroy (parts) of the plant. Cyberattacks can cause unwanted and unexpected results. The consequences of a cyberattack on a chemical facility could be disastrous. The Nitro attacks in particular showed that chemical plants are considered a target. In the same time as the Nitro attack sessions, several other hacker groups have also begun targeting some of the same chemical companies. They send malicious PDF and DOC files, which use exploits to drop variants of "Backdoor.Sogu". This particular threat was also used by hackers to compromise a Korean social network site to steal records of 35 million users.

---

[9] This application is freely available from poisonivy-rat.com. It comes fully loaded with a number of plug-ins to give an attacker complete control of the compromised computer.

Fortunate, no cyber-attack on chemical facilities has resulted in releases of toxic chemicals. That does not mean that it will not happen in the future. With recent developments in mind, and considering the types of chemicals stored in chemical plants, such as chlorine and nitrous oxide, it seems clear that creating, adopting, implementing and adhering to safety and security guidelines is extremely important to prevent catastrophes. Strengthening safety and security at chemical plant sites, including the information network, is an important task in preventing the hostile use of chemicals. Therefore, it is very important to (continue to) advance the protection mechanisms of chemical plants' computer networks in order to reduce vulnerabilities.

Countering Cyber-Attacks

The discovery of recent viruses exposed serious knowledge gaps in how cyber security is implemented and maintained by companies. Cyber security includes the overall coordinated measures and actions taken by potential targets to prevent, prepare, analyse, and respond to the threats their (information) systems are facing due to cyber-attacks. Objectives include protecting the confidentiality, integrity, and processes. As argued before, the majority of chemical companies have done little or nothing with cyber security to guard the safety and security of their processes. They should start by assessing their potential for being hit by cyber-attacks and identifying their strengths and weaknesses. It is also important to map the "connection policy"; how are systems and networks connected to each other? What measures have been taken to prevent infiltration of the system? What are the standards and demands for both internal and external operations? Once companies have a thorough understanding of their current level of security, once can determine where vulnerabilities exist and what actions need to be taken to address them. Protective measures can be developed and applied to reduce vulnerabilities, system threats, and their consequences. Finally, one could create an integral security policy for the facility's information network.

Some of the most serious security issues facing ICS applications include: increased connectivity; interdependencies; complexity; and system accessibility. These issues can be used to exploit vulnerabilities that can be found in different components needed to run a plant's processes, including hardware and software, network communications, structures and configurations, service providers, and users and operators. The most appealing targets are those components that are easily accessible. Therefore, one should at least install decent gateway security; software that includes scanning incoming data for malware and viruses, but also intrusion detection and prevention systems.[10] The latest protective monitoring

---

[10] The UK Intelligence Agency GCHQ, for instance, estimates that 80 % of the cyber-attacks can be dealt with by better computer 'hygiene'.

systems can provide effective defences against the majority of attacks. A major disadvantage of protection software, however, is that it is usually reactive. It needs to be updated constantly and is often not prepared to identify new threats. Therefore, a more active and profound security approach might be needed; one that is also able to detect and respond to those attacks that managed to defeat the first line of protective measures. Maintaining aggressive and proactive cyber security, however, will require a strong and enduring commitment of resources, clear incentives, and close collaboration with all stakeholders.

Experts offer various recommendations to address vulnerabilities; security programs that consider all possible infection pathways and have strategies for mitigating those pathways should be adopted. These systems should also; 'Recognize that no protective security posture is perfect and take steps to aggressively segment control networks to limit the consequences of an incursion; Install ICS-appropriate intrusion detection technologies to spot attacks and raise an alarm when equipment is compromised or at risk of compromise; Deploy, operate and maintain at maximum effectiveness ICS-appropriate security technologies and practices—these include firewalls, antivirus technology, patching systems and whitelisting designed for SCADA and ICS, to make attacks by sophisticated malware much more difficult; Look beyond traditional network-layer firewalls to firewalls capable of deep packet inspection of key SCADA and ICS protocols; Focus on securing last-line-of-defence critical systems, particularly safety integrated systems; Include security assessments and testing as part of the system-development and periodic maintenance processes followed by correction of identified potential vulnerabilities, thereby decreasing the likelihood of a successful attack'. It is also uttered to include mandatory encryption of computer data in SCADA-controlled utilities transmission and distribution systems.

It is virtually impossible to create a system that can counter any attempt of intrusion. Even if one would limit access to the internet by creating "air gaps", barriers physically separating the plant's electronic equipment from the outside world, the system would not be fully secure. For example, the Natanz nuclear facility is a massive and well-protected nuclear site in the middle of the desert in central Iran, not connected to the internet, yet, it was effected by Stuxnet. It is believed that an infected thumb drive or laptop was plugged into the system by an employee working at the site. Besides identifying vulnerabilities and taking precautionary measures to counter the threats, the most important step in plant security is probably creating a "security/responsibility culture" among all staff members, including management. A facility needs educated staff that is observant; people who mind security rules and keep a close eye on the running processes, carefully look after the machinery. Staff should be on the lookout for abnormal or suspect behaviour, including of colleagues, for instance, when one escalates access privileges. The safety culture that has emerged in the chemical industry over the last 20 years can be used as a model for such a security culture. With their sophisticated risk-management cultures, BP, Exxon, and Shell in the oil and gas sector and Dow Chemicals and DuPont in chemicals exemplify how a safety culture can become a security culture.

As exploitation of system vulnerabilities could very well transcend individual company interests, potentially becoming a(n) (inter)national risk, it is beneficial for both industry as well as National Authorities to support initiatives that could reduce the threat. The US seems to be taking the lead in this regard, providing a range of different products aimed at improving cyber security at chemical facilities, varying from issuing documents to providing free or low-cost trainings. Examples include: the 'Chemical Sector Training Resources Guide', which contains a list of different initiatives to assist facility security officers in training their staff on cyber security awareness among others; the Chemical Sector Awareness Guide, which intends to assist owners and operators to take security measures against threats presented by explosive weapons and cyber vulnerabilities; and the Chemical Sector Monthly Suspicious Activity Calls, which can update employees of chemical companies, associations, and agencies on physical and cyber threats to chemical infrastructure.[11] There are also the biannual National Cyber Exercises to improve the capabilities of the cyber incident response community; encourage the advancement of public–private partnerships within the critical infrastructure sectors; and strengthen relationships between the Federal Government and partners at the state, local, and international levels.

Another valuable tool is The Roadmap to Secure Control Systems in the Chemical Sector, which describes a plan for voluntary improving cyber security in the chemical sector.[12]. It proposes a framework for investing in control system security risk mitigation efforts and action toward improving defences against cyber events that could disrupt operations. The Roadmap is a result of a collaboration between chemical sector stakeholders, such as the Chemical Sector Coordinating Council and owners and operators of chemical facilities, and government agencies. Chemical industry has produced other tools that address cyber security as well. For instance, safeguarding information and process control systems is an essential part of The Responsible Care Security Code of the American Chemistry Council.[13] It incorporates guidance to assist chemical industry to address their cyber security management programs. There is an equivalent to this Code, developed to address chemical industry in Europe: the European Responsible Care Security Code.[14]

Most initiatives to increase cyber security at chemical plants are voluntary in nature. Only a minority of industries in a minority of countries are forced to guard the safety of its processes by regulation. At present, the US regulates systems' security only for the commercial nuclear-power industry and, to a much lesser

---

[11] These are all initiatives by the US's Department of Homeland Security. To obtain a copy of the documents, or for more information, contact: http://www.ChemicalSector@dhs.gov.

[12] For the Roadmap, check.http://www.us-cert.gov/control_systems/pdf/ChemSec_Roadmap.pd f. For more information, see http://www.chemicalcybersecurity.org/

[13] For more information, check: http://responsiblecare.americanchemistry.com/Responsible-Care-Program-Elements/Responsible-Care-Security-Code/default.aspx.

[14] Available at: http://www.cefic.org/Documents/ResponsibleCare/Feuillet%20RC_Security Code_V4.pdf.

extent, the chemical industry.[15] Yet, most of critical infrastructure is privately owned and extremely vulnerable to a highly sophisticated cyber weapon like Stuxnet. The desirability of a state-centric approach, however, is subject to debate. One disagrees about whether the government should be allowed to require the owners of critical infrastructure to improve the security of their computer networks. Any expansion of government into private-sector security will raise a host of concerns, including issues of privacy, innovation, and legality.

Opponents suggest a flexible dialogue that includes a wide range of participants from the technical community, the private sector, government, and the user/consumer groups. Government and industry, they argue, should develop security standards and best practices collaboratively rather than top-down prescriptions from regulators. Proponents of government regulations, on the other hand, argue that voluntary action, information sharing, and public–private partnerships is no longer sufficient. The abilities of individual critical infrastructure owners to undertake cyber security will be uneven, with some companies doing better than others. Without a set of concrete government incentives or enforceable regulations, corporations will continue to make risk-management decisions based on their self-interest, which does not necessarily account for larger national security concerns. It is for this reason that the US has law mandating minimum cyber security standards for critical infrastructure going through Congress.[16] In the UK, similar measures are also under construction.

Possible OPCW Involvement in Cyber Security for Chemical Plants

Policymakers and business leaders see a need to "bridge the gap" between the independent cyber security demands of commercial enterprise and the collective security imperatives of a nation protecting its vital infrastructure, but they do not agree on the means to tackle the problem. This could provide opportunities for the Organisation for the Prohibition of Chemical Weapons (OPCW). The OPCW

---

[15] For instance, in late 2006, US Congress passed a law that gave the Department of Homeland Security (DHS) the authority to regulate the US's highest risk chemical facilities and directs DHS to develop chemical facility security regulation. On 9 April 2007, the DHS published the Chemical Facility Anti-Terrorism Standards (CFATS) in response (available at http://www.dhs.gov/files/programs/gc_1169501486179.shtm).

[16] Remarkable in this respect is the fact that the US Bill that sought to protect computer networks running the power grid, gas pipelines and water supply and transportation systems from hackers by creating a set of security standards for companies to meet, known as the Cybersecurity Act of 2012, was voted down by the Senate on Thursday 2 August 2012, despite warnings that hackers could shut down critical infrastructure with the click of a mouse. Republicans opposed the Bill, siding with business lobbyists who claimed that any security standards, even voluntary ones, would unfairly saddle business with cositly regulations. This means that key US national security legislation will likely not be addressed until 2013.

could, for instance, act as a "broker" between industry and Member States and explore what steps can be taken collectively. It could provide a platform where all stakeholders come together to search for solutions to tackle the problem. States could be tempted by this idea because working within the framework of an international organisation will significantly enhance cost-effectiveness. Industry, on the other hand, might cooperate because rules that will apply to all facilities will "level playing fields". Furthermore, many of the chemical industries are international with international suppliers, manufacturers, and costumers and cyber-attacks are cross-border phenomena. It is an international problem, but it lacks an international response. Under the auspices of the OPCW, governments and industry can take a lead in creating (a) groundbreaking initiative(s) which could improve defences at chemical plants.

In May 2012, a brainstorming session on chemical safety and security took place at the OPCW headquarters, involving the members of the recently established Task Force on Chemical Safety and Security and representatives of a major, leading chemical company. The latter indeed argued that the OPCW can play a major role as a facilitator between governments, industry, and other stakeholders and that, considering its broad network and close ties with governments, the OPCW could gain an important position within the sphere of chemical security. It could play a managerial role in determining the industries weaknesses and strengths and filling those gaps. Similar thoughts were put forward during, for instance, a meeting conducted on 7 and 8 June 2012, in an informal setting at the OPCW Headquarters, which provided a forum for discussions and exchanges of ideas between experts from all regions.

In the framework of Project V—Preparedness of States Parties to prevent and respond to attacks involving chemicals—of the European Council Decision of 23 March 2012, the OPCW's Office of Special Projects (OSP) is in fact working on an activity entitled 'OPCW as a platform for enhancing security at chemical plants'. The activity is meant to 'identify opportunities and requirements for follow-up measures to further the process of enhancing chemical security, and for developing the OPCW as a platform for exchanges on this matter. A result of the project will be a series of practical proposals for how the OPCW can be further developed as a platform for cooperation and coordination in the area of chemical security'. The OPCW becoming "the place to go to" for all relevant stakeholders would be a step forward in building better relationships and promoting synergies, and could provide the opportunity to share information and best practices, including regarding evolving cyber threats.

Although cyber security is not a part of the OPCW's focus yet, as it is an important part of the overall security approach at chemical plants, it should not be ignored. The framework of Project V certainly provides an opportunity to explore this topic. The fact that the OPCW is repeatedly urged to promote/enhance already existing safety and security programs rather than creating new ones by both National Authorities and industry, however, could be a stumbling block. They also emphasise that the OPCW should avoid any duplication of efforts. In particular in the area of chemical safety, there are several international agencies and organisations that have partial mandates and undertake certain activities. Therefore, the OSP has started to create reference booklets with a collection of existing programs, mechanisms, and initiatives.[17] From this research, it appears that there is neither a leading international entity on chemical security in general nor one with particular focus on cyber security for chemical plants. The OPCW could step into this vacuum.

For starters, the OPCW could develop and issue self-assessment forms with which chemical facilities can assess their level of security in general, including vulnerabilities in the information network.[18] Such "evaluation forms" could be used as a means for promoting, developing, and sustaining improved overall level of security, including cyber security at chemical plants. The forms could be distributed amongst random facilities (for instance, in a pilot project). One could monitor whether any action is taken to improve vulnerabilities that are identified after completing the forms. Eventually, a database could be created were chemical facilities can (voluntary) upload their results and the measures taken to address weaknesses in the system (for instance, on a yearly basis). The OPCW could be the host of such a database.

Transparency of good safety and security performance at a number of chemical plants would pressure other facilities to perform well on these issues as well (because no-one likes to be known as the 'weakest link'). Furthermore, if facilities will indeed upload their results, findings, and improvements in the database, it could be used by (smaller) entities to request advice and/or assistance from other, more advanced facilities that may have better scores on specific security aspects. These companies may search the database to find facilities that perform better/best on the particular issue they would like to address. As such, the database will also be a tool for sharing information and best practices on the issue of cyber security at chemical plants. This initiative could contribute to a better level of cyber security at chemical facilities without imposing (new) rules and regulations.

The OPCW could raise awareness of cyber threats and promote a (more) holistic approach to the problem, by encouraging firms to share information about the threats they have identified. If this proves to be a success, eventually, it could result in relevant authorities, or chemical industry itself, requesting certain regulations in this area. Protocols for trusted information sharing could be created and perhaps even lead to obligations to disclose information. Ultimately, mechanisms for reviewing progress made regarding the prevention of cyber-attacks on chemical plants, including advancement of anti-cyber measures, and reviews of attacks that have been perpetrated—in an incident reporting system[19]—could be created under the auspices of the OPCW in the future.

---

[17] For more information, contact: Mr. K. Paturej, Director OSP, email: krzysztof.paturej@msz.gov.pl .

[18] In the nuclear area some efforts in this respect have been made as well; for instance, IAEA Evaluation Worksheets or NUREG/CR-6847, "Cyber Security Self-Assessment Method for U.S. Nuclear Power Plants".

[19] For instance, the US National Cyber Security Division has established a mechanism to report vulnerabilities and incidents. Available at: https://forms.us-cert.gov/report/.

Summary and Conclusions

Vulnerabilities in industrial control systems are of high concern. Modern critical infrastructure facilities rely on computer hardware and software to monitor and control equipment that supports numerous industrial processes, including chemical production. With codes of viruses like Stuxnet, Duqu, Flame, Night Dragon, and Nitro in the open, even actors with limited financial and technical resources have the capability to compromise high-value targets. A successful infiltration could lead to cyber espionage if attackers would steal valuable information. Experts claim that cyber-attacks can degrade or stop the operation of a critical infrastructure facility that delivers essential utility, or affect multiple facilities due to the interdependent nature of the infrastructure sectors responsible for providing essential services. Although viruses such as Stuxnet have opened the eyes of experts and governments to destructive possibilities of a new type of covert attacks, industry and companies do not seem ready to counter them (yet). In many countries, policy lacks a coherent approach to protecting critical digital assets outside of the government and, in most cases, relies on voluntary participation of private industry. Cyber security policy must further evolve as critical gaps remain, including the incomplete protection of digital infrastructure vital to national security. The OPCW might be an a position to contribute to better cyber security at chemical plants. It could provide a platform where all stakeholder can come together and take a lead in creating initiatives that could improve cyber defences at chemical plants.

Bibliography

M.M. Ahlers, Inside a government computer attack exercise. CNN. (2011). http://edition.cnn.com/2011/10/17/tech/innovation/cyberattack-exercise-idaho/index.html. Accessed 8 Apr 2013

A. Akbar Dareini, D. Murphy, Iran: 'Flame' virus fight began with oil attack. The Washington Times. (2012). http://www.washingtontimes.com/nesws/2012/may/30/computer-virus-briefly-hits-irans-oil-industry/?page=1. Accessed 8 Apr 2013

P. Beaumont, N. Hopkins, US was 'key player in cyber-attacks on Iran's nuclear programme. The Guardian. (2012). http://www.guardian.co.uk/world/2012/jun/01/obama-sped-up-cyber-attack-iran. Accessed 8 Apr 2013

W.J. Broad, J. Markoff, D.E. Sanger, Israeli test on worm called crucial in Iran nuclear delay. The New York Times. (2011). http://www.nytimes.com/2011/01/16/world/middleeast/16stuxnet.html?pagewanted=all. Accessed 8 Apr 2013

G. Burton, Boom in cyber attacks on critical infrastructure reported in the US. Computing. (2012). http://www.computing.co.uk/ctg/news/2188813/boom-cyber-attacks-critical-infra-structure-reported. Accessed 8 Apr 2013

CBS News, Stuxnet: Computer worm opens new era of warfare. (2012). http://www.cbsnews.com/video/watch/?id=7400904n&tag=contentBody;storyMediaBox. Accessed 8 Apr 2013

E. Chien, G. O'Gorman, The Nitro Attacks; Stealing secrets from the chemical industry. Symantec. (2011). http://www.symantec.com/content/en/us/enterprise/media/security_response/whitepapers/the_nitro_attacks.pdf. Accessed 8 Apr 2013

M. Clayton, Alert: major cyber attack aimed at gas pipeline industry. The Christian Science Monitor. (2012). http://www.csmonitor.com/USA/2012/0505/Alert-Major-cyber-attack-aimed-at-natural-gas-pipeline-companies. Accessed 8 Apr 2013

B. Dehghanpisheh, Attacked by "Flame": will Iran retaliate for the latest cyberassault?. Time. (2012). http://www.time.com/time/world/article/0,8599,2115970,00.html#ixzz1zfR6JQ2A. Accessed 8 Apr 2013

Department of Homeland Security Office of Cybersecurity and Communication, National Cybersecurity Division, 'Cyber Storm III', Final Report. (2011). http://www.dhs.gov/xlibrary/assets/nppd-cyber-storm-iii-final-report.pdf. Accessed 8 Apr 2012

European Union (2012) Council Decision 2012/166/CFSP of 23 March 2012

M.J. Gross, A declaration of cyber-war. Vanity Fair. (2011). http://www.vanityfair.com/culture/features/2011/04/stuxnet-201104. Accessed 8 Apr 2013

N. Hopkins, Stuxnet attack forced Britain to rethink the cyber war. The Guardian. (2011). http://www.guardian.co.uk/politics/2011/may/30/stuxnet-attack-cyber-war-iran. Accessed 8 Apr 2013

J. Hahn, D.P. Gillen, T. Anderson, Process control systems in the chemical industry: safety v. security, *20th Annual CCPS International Conference.* INL. (2005). http://www.inl.gov/technicalpublications/Documents/3169874.pdf. Accessed 8 Apr 2013

J. Halliday, Stuxnet worm is the 'work of a national government agency'. The Guardian. (2010). http://www.guardian.co.uk/technology/2010/sep/24/stuxnet-worm-national-agency. Accessed 8 Apr 2013

N. Hodge, E. Entous, Oil firms hit by hackers from China, report says. The Wall Street Journal. (2011). http://online.wsj.com/article/SB10001424052748703716904576134661111518864.html. Accessed 8 Apr 2013

G. Keizer, Hackers used "Poison Ivy" malware to steal chemical, defense secrets. Techworld. (2011). http://news.techworld.com/security/3314804/hackers-used-poison-ivy-malware-to-steal-chemical-defense-secrets/. Accessed 8 Apr 2013

P.K. Kerr, J. Rollins, C.A. Theohary, The Stuxnet computer worm: Harbinger of an emerging warfare capability. CRS Report for Congress (7-5700/R41524) Congressional Research Service. (2010). http://www.fas.org/sgp/crs/natsec/R41524.pdf. Accessed 8 Apr 2013

D. Lee, 'Flame: massive cyber-attack discovered, researchers say'. BBC News. (2012). http://www.bbc.com/news/technology-18238326. Accessed 8 Apr 2013

J. Masters, Confronting the cyber threat. Council on foreign relations. (2011). http://www.cfr.org/technology-and-foreign-policy/confronting-cyber-threat/p15577. Accessed 8 Apr 2013

McAfee, Global energy cyberattacks: "Night Dragon". McAfee Foundstone Professional Services and McAfee Labs. (2011). http://www.mcafee.com/us/resources/white-papers/wp-global-energy-cyberattacks-night-dragon.pdf. Accessed 8 Apr 2013

Newsroom, Chemicals and defence firms targeted by hacking attack. BBC News. (2011). http://www.bbc.co.uk/news/technology-15529930. Accessed 8 Apr 2013

OPCW, Opening statement by the director-general to the executive council at its sixty-ninth session, 10 July 2012, EC-69/INF.3 (2012)

S. Ottewel, Industry gets cyber-security reality check. Chemical Processing. (2011). http://www.chemicalprocessing.com/articles/2011/cyber-security-reality-check.html. Accessed 8 Apr 2013

N. Perlroth, Researchers find clues in malware. The New York Times. (2012). http://www.nytimes.com/2012/05/31/technology/researchers-link-flame-virus-to-stuxnet-and-duqu.html. Accessed 8 Apr 2013

E. Rekers, VS en Israël testten gezamenlijk Stuxnet-worm. Elsevier. (2011). http://www.elsevier.nl/web/Nieuws/Internet-Gadgets/286767/VS-en-Israel-testten-gezamenlijk-Stuxnetworm.htm. Accessed 8 Apr 2013

T. Rid, P. McBurney, Cyber-weapons. RUSI J. **157**(1), 6–13

D.E. Sanger, Obama order sped up wave of cyberattacks against Iran. The New York Times. (2012). http://www.nytimes.com/2012/06/01/world/middleeast/obama-ordered-wave-of-cyberattacks-against-iran.html?pagewanted=all. Accessed 8 Apr 2013

G. Smith, Cyber security law fails to pass senate before month-long break. The Huffington Post. (2012).   http://www.huffingtonpost.com/2012/08/02/cyber-security-law_n_1733751.html. Accessed 8 Apr 2013

Staged cyber attack reveals vulnerability in power grid. Available through Youtube. http://www.y outube.com/watch?v=fJyWngDco3g&NR=1&feature=endscreen. Accessed 8 Apr 2013

Symantec, W32.Duqu; The precursor to the next Stuxnet version 1.4. Symantec security response.   (2011).   http://www.symantec.com/content/en/us/enterprise/media/security_ response/whitepapers/w32_duqu_the_precursor_to_the_next_stuxnet.pdf. Accessed 8 Apr 2013

Symantec, What do you need to know about the 'Duqu' threat'. Symantec Security Response. (2011). http://www.symantec.com/resources/articles/article.jsp?aid=20110311_duqu_threat. Accessed 8 Apr 2013

The UK Intelligence Agency GCHQ, for instance, estimates that 80% of the cyber-attacks can be dealt with by better computer 'hygiene' (Hopkins op.cit)

US Department of Homeland Security, Roadmap to Secure Control Systems in the Chemical Sector. US-CERT. (2009). http://www.us-cert.gov/control_systems/pdf/ChemSec_Roadmap. pdf. Accessed 8 Apr 2013

K. Vick, Finder of flame virus tells Israel to stop before it's too late. Time. (2012). http://world. time.com/2012/06/06/finder-of-flame-virus-warns-israel-to-stop-before-its-too-late/

From Fortress to Resilience

Sandro Bologna, Alessandro Fasani and Maurizio Martellini

Abstract *"From Fortress to Resilience"* written by Maurizio Martellini, Sandro Bologna and Alessandro Fasani, outlines firstly the need for differentiating approaches between dealing with cyber attacks against critical infrastructures, that must be dealt by engineers, and cyber attacks against government infrastructures and institutions, that must be dealt by the intelligence. The paper then focuses on the imperative of moving from a "fortress" to a "resilience" approach, that's to say from a preventive, passive defense to an holistic one that can adapt to diverse cyber attacks and can recover and recover quickly when systems are damaged.

At present too many people use to talk about cyber security with different meanings, ranging from cyber attacks addressing single SCADA (Supervisory Control And Data Acquisition) Systems to cyber attacks addressing *sovereign states*. These attacks cannot be treated with the same tools and by the same organizations. In case of cyber attacks to industrial systems and more in general to critical infrastructures, it is mostly a technical problem that should be addressed by engineers, while in the case of cyber attacks to a *sovereign state* it must be regulated as a warfare act that should be addressed by the *intelligence*.

Among the different source of data we may refer to the ICS-CERT Report for the first category, covering reports coming from different sectors spanning to

S. Bologna (✉)
IWG and Italian Association of Critical Infrastructures' Experts, Rome, Italy
e-mail: s.gaycken@fu-berlin.de

A. Fasani
Landau Network-Centro Volta, Como, Italy
e-mail: alessandro.fasani@centrovolta.it

M. Martellini
IWG and Landau Network-Centro Volta, Como, Italy
e-mail: maurizio.martellini@centrovolta.it

M. Martellini (ed.), *Cyber Security*, SpringerBriefs in Computer Science,
DOI: 10.1007/978-3-319-02279-6_5, © The Author(s) 2013

energy, water, dams, nuclear, chemical, government and critical infrastructure. The Report gives an idea of the growing algorithm passing from nine reported incidents in 2009, to 41 in 2010 to 198 last year. These incidents highlight the activity of sophisticated threat actors and their ability to gain access to system networks, avoid detection, use advanced techniques to maintain a presence. Unfortunately, there is no *"silver bullet"* solution in the horizon.

For the second category, cyber attacks to *sovereign states*, a set of nations have publically developed and published their National Cyber Security Strategies (NCSS) or, alternatively named, National Information Security Strategies; among others Australia, Canada, United States, France, Germany, but not Italy. The first and most important problem we may notice by cross reading the different NCSS is the lack of a common understanding of the term *cyber security*. The lack of a common definition across nations may be a cause of confusion between them when discussing international approaches to the global cyberspace threats. Another problem is the understanding of the term warfare attack, in the cyber domain and the concept of cyber deterrence, if any. The military have started to use the term cyber-war, but it has nothing to do with the conventional war, and with the Mutual Assured Destruction (MAD) policy of the Cold War, because the initiators of a cyber attack may remain largely unknown, operating under the specific umbrella of a *sovereign state* or even supported by *rouge states*. On August 10th, 2012, The Washington Post reported *"The Pentagon has proposed that military cyber-specialists be given permission to take action outside its computer networks to defend critical U.S. computer systems to prevent the potential for a cyber attack to damage power stations, water-treatment plants and other critical systems—a move that officials say would set a significant precedent"*. It is clear that the cyber-war is also among different institutional bodies belonging to the same *sovereign state*.

We believe that there are too many interests to ride this new subject but very little step heads. Every year the number of cyber incidents is growing in all different areas. Security strategies are confused and different industries providing cyber technologies are pushing to sell their products without a global vision of the problem. Over the past years, the rise of our interconnected, interdependent society combined with terrorist attacks and natural disasters has posed new challenges to the community of critical infrastructure protection. Our proposal is to move on from the concept of "fortress" to the concept of "resilience".

An acceptable definition of the Fortress Approach is "an approach in which every acceptable precaution is taken to disaster proof a system or service".

An acceptable definition of the Resilience Approach is "the ability of a system or service to resist the effects of a disruptive event, or to recover from the effects of a disruptive event to a normal or near-normal state". The requirement for resilience is based on the premise that protective, preventive, and deterrent safeguards will not always be effective (i.e. successful in keeping out a threat) and therefore will require response, recovery, and restorative action.

The problem of classify all possible threats and scenarios has been covered in different projects, but always these classifications have been passed by the reality (Stuxnet and Fukushima are just the two most popular examples). To classify all possible cyber threats and physical threats is an endless job that historically has shown all its limits: it works only for a short time.

Many of the failures in critical systems are due to failure of the assumptions in the used command-and-control paradigm. The command-and-control paradigm normally used is underlain by four flawed assumptions: (i) a focus on average conditions and particular time and space scales; (ii) a belief that problems arising from different causes in these systems do not interact; (iii) an expectation that change will be incremental and linear, and (iv) an assumption that keeping the system in some particular state will maximize yield, indefinitely.

An alternative approach, based on resilience, assumes instead that critical systems behave as complex adaptive systems able to adapt to the different circumstances. Enhancing the resilience of a system can be achieved through the appropriate combination of security measures to address intentional and accidental incidents; business continuity practices to deal with disruptions and ensure the continuation of essential services; and emergency management planning to ensure adequate response procedures are in place to deal with unforeseen disruptions and natural disasters.

Moving from the Fortress Approach to the Resilience Approach requires changes in all aspects of the Systems, both technical and organizational. Identifying and ameliorating all aspects of the "system operation" for a "large complex infrastructure" is a challenging task because a "large complex infrastructure" is in fact a concatenation of many different sub-systems tied together by a variety of physical and procedural connections. This will become more and more challenging with the increasing penetration of the concepts of system-of-systems. It describes the large-scale integration of many independent, self-contained systems in order to satisfy a global need. While specific problems will require specific expertise, the common characteristics of all these large, complex problems is that they require a multidisciplinary approach.

At the present the European Commission through the European Network and Information Security Agency (ENISA) is very active in establishing scientific foundations for the concept of resilience applied to Critical Information Infrastructures (CII), and also possible metrics.

Last but not least, from an academic pointy of view, there are conceptual similarities between the international community efforts to secure dual-use intangibles (like expertise and sensitive knowledge) and cybersecurity. As a consequence of that, it could be interesting to explore for the cyber domain the adoption of International Codes of Conduct developed, for instance, in sensitive CBRN areas.

Bibliography

ENISA, Enabling and managing end-to-end resilience. ENISA report (2011), http://www.enisa.europa.eu/activities/identity-and-trust/library/deliverables/e2eres. Accessed 28 Mar 2013
ENISA, Activities (2013a), http://www.enisa.europa.eu/activities/Resilience-and-CIIP/Incidents%20reporting/metrics/metrics. Accessed 28 Mar 2013

ENISA, The European network and information security agency (2013b), http://www.enisa.
europa.eu/. Accessed 28 Mar 2013

Industrial Defender, White paper: seven best practices for automation system cyber security and
compliance (2012), http://www.isssource.com/wp-content/uploads/2012/05/053012Industrial-
Defender-Seven-Best-Practices.pdf. Accessed 28 Mar 2013

R. Larson et al., The 3 R's of critical energy networks: reliability, robustness and resil-
iency: a white paper submitted to the MIT energy research council. Mit Edu. (2005),
http://cesf.mit.edu/papers/ThreeRs.pdf. Accessed 28 Mar 2013

E. Nakashima, Pentagon proposes more robust role for its cyber-specialists. The Washington post
(2012),   http://www.washingtonpost.com/world/national-security/pentagon-proposes-more-
robust-role-for-its-cyber-specialists/2012/08/09/1e3478ca-db15-11e1-9745-d9ae6098d493_
story.html?wpisrc=nl_tech. Accessed 28 Mar 2013

US Department of Homeland Security: ICS-CERT Incident Response Summary Report
2009–2011 (2012), http://scadahacker.com/library/Documents/ICS_Events/ICS-CERT%20
Incident%20Response%20Summary%20Report.pdf. Accessed 28 Mar 2013

B. Walker, A resilience approach to integrated assessment. Integr. Assess. J. 5(1), 77–97 (2005)

Cyber Security and Resilience of Industrial Control Systems and Critical Infrastructures

Sandro Bologna, Alessandro Fasani and Maurizio Martellini

Abstract *"Cyber Security And Resilience Of Industrial Control Systems And Critical Infrastructures"*, written by Maurizio Martellini, Sandro Bologna and Alessandro Fasani, it's a natural follow-up of the previous paper and describes what Industrial Control Systems are, provides an analysis on what are the main vulnerabilities affecting ICS and describes the principal methodologies for attacking them. Then, the paper defines what measures could be taken in order to make ICS and Critical Infrastructures resilient. The document ends outlining what international measures are being taken in order to protect critical infrastructure and their systems.

Introduction

In the past few years, many countries and companies have come to understand that critical infrastructures can be attacked via cyberspace with serious consequences. Viruses and malwares can be used as weapons aimed at the disruption of critical infrastructure systems.

Needless to say, Stuxnet was the starting point of the escalation in the number and in the sophistication of cyberattacks in the last three years. According to a research carried out in 2012 the number of vulnerabilities in SCADA (Supervisory Control and Data Acquisition) systems detected between 2010 and 2012 is twenty times higher compared to the 2005–2010 period. This makes it possible to divide the

S. Bologna (✉)
IWG and Italian Association of Critical Infrastructures' Experts, Rome, Italy
e-mail: s.bologna@infrastrutturecritiche.it

A. Fasani · M. Martellini
IWG and Landau Network—Centro Volta, Como, Italy
e-mail: alessandro.fasani@centrovolta.it

M. Martellini
e-mail: maurizio.martellini@centrovolta.it

M. Martellini (ed.), *Cyber Security*, SpringerBriefs in Computer Science,
DOI: 10.1007/978-3-319-02279-6_6, © The Author(s) 2013

age of cyber security in Before Stuxnet and After Stuxnet. Although it may sound redundant, it's really important to stress the fact that this malware was a game changer. Not only in the structure of the malware, more complex than ever before, but also in the nature of the perpetrators and of the targets. These differences have profound implications. Since Stuxnet industrial plants and infrastructures owners have become aware that the cyberspace is an unruled and uncharted global common where war can be conducted with less destructive results, compared to physical war, but with high disruptive potential. The second aspect to underline is that the words ICS and SCADA have gone under the spotlight. Another point that is really important to stress is the difference between an Industrial Control System and a commercial Operating System. Both can be targets of cyberattacks, but they have different nature and so the attacks and the consequences. One of the main differences is that Operating Systems such as Microsoft Windows or Apple Mac OSX are available to anyone and so relatively easy to study and analyze, due to the wider audience of consumers and users. ICS are a different thing. They are more difficult to acquire since they serve a limited scope of consumers, mainly industrials, and in order to perform an attack on those, a deep practical knowledge on both hardware and software is needed; also it is worth mentioning that there are multiple producers and vendors, differencing system from system. In contrast to a cyberattack against retail operating systems that is widespread because many systems and networks depend on them—Windows or Mac OSX, for example—and their flaws, an attack to a specific Industrial Control System is based on a deep knowledge on that specific system, with its own peculiarities.

Retail Operating Systems are more likely to be attacked, thus more attention in fixing their vulnerabilities is given, on the contrary, Industrial Control Systems and its components were almost never attacked before Stuxnet. For this reason, vulnerabilities were rarely studied and therefore fixed. It is worth mentioning, as a supporting example, that one of the exploited vulnerabilities used in the Stuxnet attack was discovered in May 2005 and fixed after the attack, five years later.

The attack against the Natanz nuclear enrichment plant showed that a nuclear enrichment process inside a facility can be altered from miles away through a malware. The operation Olympic Games clearly demonstrate that nation states have become fully aware of the potential of the digital weapon. From this, we can conclude that since 2010 the attention towards Industrial Control Systems and their components has raised considerably both in the potential attackers minds and in the persons in charge of the security of those infrastructures' systems. For this reason there is the need not only to defend them, but also to make the infrastructures able to withstand and recover from an attack, that's to say to make them resilient.

Industrial Control Systems

"Industrial Control Systems (ICS) are an integral part of the industrial infrastructure providing for the national good. These systems include Distributed Control Systems (DCS) Supervisory Control and Data Acquisition systems (SCADA), Programmable Logic

Controllers (PLC), and devices such as Remote Telemetry Units (RTU), smart meters, and intelligent field instruments including remotely programmable valves and intelligent electronic relays. While sharing basic constructs with Information Technology (IT) business systems, ICSs are technically, administratively, and functionally more complex and unique than business IT systems."

Industrial control systems and their components control different infrastructures, from energy production, to manufacturing and water treatment. Given that ICS is a general term, we could split it in its different hardware and software components:

- Supervisory Control and Data Acquisition system or Distributed Control Systems.
- Human Machine Interface.
- Programmable Logic Controllers.
- Generic hardware and software.

A SCADA system it's a centralized system that monitors and controls entire sites, or multiple, interconnected systems over large areas. Most control actions are performed generally by PLCs that, for example, control the flow of cooling water through part of an industrial process, but the SCADA system may also allow operators to change the set points for the flow, and enable alarm conditions, such as loss of flow and high temperature, to be displayed and recorded. It is straightforward that, tampering with the SCADA system and/or the PLCs, could result in severe consequences. A Human Machine Interface it is generally a device such as a console that permits the interaction between a human operator and the machine. It allows the control and the monitoring of the running processes.

It's straightforward to say that being able to control any part of the Industrial Control Systems permits the manipulation of the mechanisms of an infrastructure (Fig. 1).

Vulnerabilities

Each ICS component has its own vulnerabilities and could be subject to a cyberattack. Between 2005 and 2012 the experts found that SCADA systems and Human Machine Interfaces are among the most targeted components of the industrial control systems (Fig. 2).

It shouldn't be difficult to understand why. Altering a SCADA system and the programmable logic controllers of an infrastructure means to take control of the infrastructure itself. Tampering with this machinery that is supposedly connected to centrifuges, gas/oil pipes, water treatment plants could result mainly in the disruption of the infrastructure and other severe consequences.

As stated in the introduction, the number of discovered vulnerabilities increased. But it is not all bad news, as the majority of vendors fixes and releases patches for most of their vulnerable ICS. Vulnerabilities are primarily detected in

SEVEN-LAYER PHYSICAL ICS ARCHITECTURE

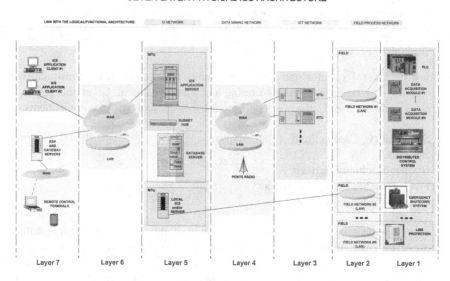

Fig. 1 Seven layer physical ICS architecture (from ESTEC JLS/2007/D1/22 Final Report (2012), ICS and smart grids security standards, guidelines and recommendations. Presented at ERNCIP conference 2012)

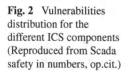

Fig. 2 Vulnerabilities distribution for the different ICS components (Reproduced from Scada safety in numbers, op.cit.)

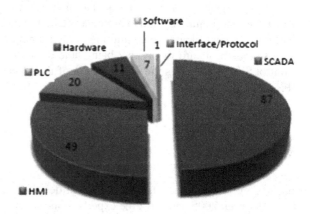

the most common products and eliminated soon. One on five vulnerability wasn't fixed soon enough (within 30 days from the discovery) or not even fixed. 65 % of these vulnerabilities is rated of "high" or "critical" severity. A value that is much higher in comparison to commercial Operating systems. It is straightforward that, for security reasons, thirty days to fix a "high" or "critical" vulnerability is a risk that should be avoided. Once a vulnerability is open for everyone to be analyzed on the internet, every critical infrastructure that uses that vulnerable component is in danger of being attacked. This attack it is most likely to end well because there is no defense provided against it.

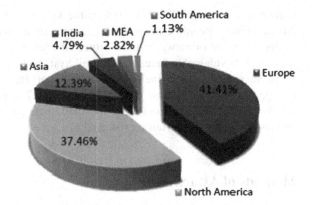

Fig. 3 ICS available from the internet distributed per macro-regions (Reproduced from Scada Safety in numbers, op.cit.)

Industrial Control Systems are normally a long lasting technology suffering from a number of "dormant" vulnerabilities that are not known to the wide public because (a) they are less likely to suffer from cyberattacks compared to retail Operative Systems; and (b) companies that receive a cyberattack tend not to divulge the fact in order not to show vulnerability or cause distrust in the stakeholders. The main problem is that Industrial Control Systems can be searched and found on the internet. Apart from the major search engine available, there are also specific databases such as ShodanHQ that map online devices (such as routers, power plants, wind turbines etc.) on the internet. From these databases we can obtain information on the characteristics of one specific system, such as the model of the hardware and the version of the software it runs. Through these methods available to everyone, experts found that Europe, as a macro-region, detains the highest number of Industrial Control Systems available from the internet (41.41 %) with Italy in first place in terms of allocations of ICS 6.8 % (Fig. 3).

As far as vulnerabilities—related to configuration management and updates installation—are concerned, still according to this research, Europe has the highest percentage of vulnerable ICS systems (54 %), with Switzerland leading the

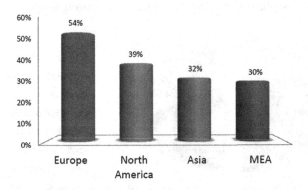

Fig. 4 Percentage of vulnerable ICS systems per macro-regions (Reproduced from Scada Safety in numbers, op.cit.)

European chart with 100 % of vulnerable systems of those available from the internet. Czech Republic in second place with 86 % and Sweden in third (67 %). Under this point of view, the most protected country in Europe is Germany, with only 20 % of vulnerable Industrial Control Systems (Fig. 4).

These samples don't include the entirety of Industrial Control Systems in Europe, so we cannot draw certain conclusions. The real problem is that cyber attacks constitute a new frontier for most risk managers and they are not prepared to consider cyber attacks during risk analysis.

Methods of Attack

Methodologies for attacking Industrial Control Systems and their components are various in nature and consequences. The most common vulnerabilities are: buffer overflow, those concerning lacks in authentication and key management, remote code execution and local privilege escalation (Fig. 5).

As we can see from the chart above, among these vulnerabilities, more than a third (36 %) is due to buffer overflow. The "buffer" is a transitional memory built in order to speed up IT processes, and has a given dedicated amount of space. "Overflowing" the buffer means to input more data than the buffer can receive, resulting not only in incapacitating a program but also to execute arbitrary code in the system. A solution to this problem could be reviewing all the codes and test them against overflowing.

Authentication/Key Management is the second cause of vulnerability. Poor passwords and authentication policies, could lead external actors to log into the systems with the same privilege of a normal user. Infrastructures should develop protected procedures and authentication requirements. User credentials should be difficult to acquire or pass through an encrypted channel. These means include systems for the recognition of biometric features, such as fingerprints, face, iris and dynamics of signing or voice.

Remote code execution is a consequence of having access into the system through the methods described above, for example. Once gained privileges, an attacker

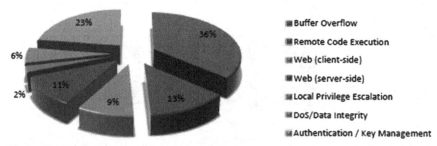

Fig. 5 Distribution of most common vulnerabilities (Reproduced from Scada Safety in numbers, op.cit.)

could escalate them until the administrator level and give arbitrary commands to the machine.

Sector Analysis

The United States Industrial Control Systems Cyber Emergency Response Team (ICS-CERT) performed a research on the 2009–2012 period to see the trends in cyberattacks as regards the sectors that have been attacked.

In 2009, the number of reported incidents was nine. The most attacked sectors were Water (3.34 %) and Energy (3.33 %) (Fig. 6).

In 2010 the number of reported incidents increased forty-one, with Energy as the leading sector with the 18.44 % of the total attacked. In 2010 the Nuclear sector was among those attacked with 5.12 % due to the discovery of Stuxnet (Fig. 7).

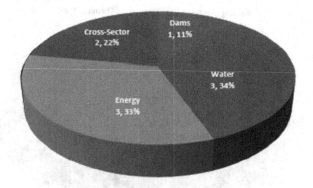

Fig. 6 Incident reports by sector (2009) (Reproduced from Scada Safety in numbers, op.cit.)

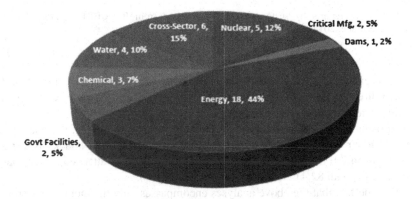

Fig. 7 Incident reports by sector (2010) (Reproduced from Scada Safety in numbers, op.cit.)

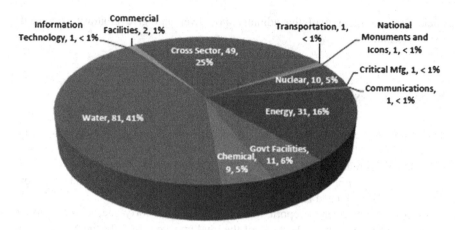

Fig. 8 Incident reports by sector (2011) (Reproduced from Scada Safety in numbers, op.cit.)

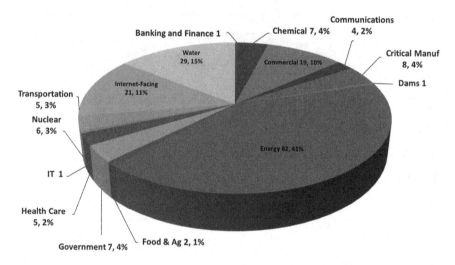

Fig. 9 Incident reports by sector (2012) (Reproduced from ICS-CERT Monthly Monitor October–December 2012)

At the end of 2011 the reported incidents skyrocketed to 198, with 81.41 % of them directed to the Water sector, followed by Energy, Nuclear, Government Facilities and Chemical (Fig. 8).

Surprisingly, according to the ICS-CERT Operational Review of the fiscal year 2012 (October 2011–September 2012) the number of reported attacks is almost the same as in 2011, but with a complete change in the most attacked sector, that's to say energy, with 82.41 % of the total reports (Fig. 9).

Given the fact that the above analyses encompasses only the incident reports of cyber attacks towards Critical Infrastructures that took place in the United States, it's not possible to draw any general conclusion. However it's interesting to point out how the number of incidents related to cyber attacks, and also the sectors involved, increased substantially from 2010 onwards.

History of Some Cases

This brief history of cyber attacks against Industrial Control Systems from 2010 until today is based on when a particular attack has been discovered, not necessarily when it started. In fact, some of these discoveries happened years after the attack started and after gigabytes of data have been stolen or the infrastructure has been disrupted. That's not entirely bad news, as at least the attacks have been discovered and security companies can analyze them, securing the flaws they exploit and learning their trends.

Producing a comprehensive list of cyberattacks is not an easy task because, generally, government agencies/national critical infrastructures/large-scale laboratories and other critical actors do not tend to disclose whether a cyberattack has taken place neither the details of it. Still this history of events can help in understanding the trend in the cyberspace of the last three years, and maybe examples of what could happen to critical infrastructures without a cyber resilience approach and without resilient Industrial Control Systems.

2010 Olympic Games: "U.S. and Israeli intelligence operation, started under President George W. Bush and expanded under President Barack Obama. President Obama secretly ordered increasingly sophisticated attacks on the computer systems that run Iran's main nuclear enrichment facilities, significantly expanding America's first sustained use of cyberweapons, according to participants in the program."

The attacks—allegedly—included: Stuxnet, Flame (and miniFlame) and Duqu as they all shared parts of the same code.

STUXNET

Type: DIRECT ATTACK

Objective(s): Iranian nuclear programme

"Discovered in June 2010, Stuxnet is believed to be the first malware targeted specifically at critical infrastructure systems. It's thought to have been designed to shut down centrifuges at Iran's Natanz uranium enrichment plant, where stoppages and other problems reportedly occurred around that time. The sophisticated worm spreads via USB drives and through four previously unknown holes, known as zero-day vulnerabilities, in Windows."

October 2011

Penetration Test

Type: HACKING TEST

Objective(s): Chemical facilities

"Idaho National Laboratory tested the vulnerabilities in their chemical facilities showing that they exist and can be exploited."

Fig. 10 Locations of 7,200 US key industrial control system directly linked to the internet and potentially vulnerable (Reproduced from BBC.co.uk website, courtesy of the US Department of Homeland Security)

December 2012
STUXNET

Type: DIRECT ATTACK

Objective(s): Iranian nuclear programme

"A power plant and other industries in southern Iran have been targeted by the Stuxnet computer worm, an Iranian civil defence official says. The virus targeted a power plant and some other industries in Hormozgan province. But the cyber attack has been successfully rebuffed and prevented from spreading, Iranian media report." (Fig. 10).

"The Department of Homeland Security released this map showing the locations of 7,200 key industrial control systems that appear to be directly linked to the internet and vulnerable to attack. The energy sector was the most-targeted field, with 82 attacks, and the water industry reported 29 attacks last year. Chemical plants faced seven cyber attacks, and nuclear companies reported six."

In February 2013, a critical vulnerability in the Industrial Control System called "Tridium Niagara AX Framework"—widely used by the military and hospitals—was found. Luckily, it was found by two security experts that alerted all the companies that used this specific ICS to increase their security measures. The two experts bought the system on eBay and it came provided with the documentation providing default username and password. This is a major problem because many facilities don't change the default credential leading to breaches in the system without even using a malware. Testing the system, it was found that it is vulnerable to a specific zero-day attack that permits to gain complete control of the machinery. A research on the SHODAN database, resulted in 21,000 critical infrastructure using the Niagara Control System that were visible and easily identifiable.

Could a Resilient Infrastructure Mitigate the Risks of Cyberattacks?

As the history of events showed, the number of **discovered** cyberattacks increased since the discovery of Stuxnet in 2010. On the one hand, the malware was the starting point of a whole new series of cyber attacks that, whether engaged in theft or extortion, or in disruption of the infrastructures' systems, have targeted critical infrastructures and government agencies, including CBRN related ones. This has been possible because of vulnerabilities in the Industrial Control Systems that are the core of the processes present in Critical Infrastructures. On the other hand, it is important to underline that Stuxnet was the only cyberattack that succeeded in causing real damage to an infrastructure. Nevertheless the spread in the discovery of these whole new series of malwares that target ICSs, at the basis of the numerous cyber attacks in the last three years, stressed the importance of a rethinking in the concept of security. That's where resilience comes to play. A resilient approach is an holistic set of procedures that encompasses the entire structure of an institution/business/infrastructure, from the IT part to the management, to ensure the ability to **prevent, deter, detect,** and **respond** to a cyber attack.

In order to achieve, or try to, resilient Industrial Control Systems, a rethinking of the whole system is needed, from the supply chain to the management of the system. The supply chain (the process of moving specific goods from supplier to customer) of an Industrial Control System, consists of several phases, among which there is the design, the manufacturing, the distribution, the process of the installing and put in operation, until the maintaining of the system and its decommission. Each of these phases should be reached by 'ad hoc' security. The entire lifecycle of the product should be protected, and this protection should be strengthened by strong enterprise security practices. In this light, it's important to understand that the highest risk factors in the supply chain happen during the install and operate and retire phases of the Industrial Control System, because it's in these phases that multiple vendors have an active role, for example by integrating products with other systems, or through measures aim at fixing the software with patch and updates. For this reason, it's difficult to monitor thoroughly all the process and assure total integrity. Nevertheless it is also important to maintain an inventory of assets and processes that support/are supported by the ICS. This is a problem for all countries: the evolution of the ICT industry means that many countries and global corporations now play a role in the ICT supply chain, and no country can source all components from totally 'trusted providers'. This trust is needed, however, as the promise of ICT-driven economic growth is dependent upon the core infrastructure being both secure and resilient.

Fast actions are essential to respond to an attack, thus coordination among the whole subsystems composing the infrastructure is pivotal. A risk management process should involve at first an assessment on the criticality of each part of the potential targets. Once the criticality has been set, the risks should be evaluated. A central part of the program is an analysis of the vulnerabilities of the SCADA system aimed at identifying and providing mitigation approaches for those vulnerabilities that could put these systems in danger; assessing the status of the industrial Control Systems in relation to updated industry standards; tracking level of threat and special circumstances that drive risks for the ICS; a risk management approach based on the maximum harm that could be suffered by the enterprise if the integrity of the infrastructure was lost. Holistic approach that involves the owner, IT office, risk experts such as a CERT, management. Once identified the risks, defining effective countermeasures should be taken, to reduce risks over time.

The fact is that "resilience" is a difficult status to reach for an infrastructure. It involves all the people connected to the various branches of an infrastructure and therefore it should start as a top-down method. The primary element to have for a critical infrastructure is a business continuity plan (BCP) in order to have active working processes in the event of an attack that would force the ICT systems offline. Also a contingency plan should be in place to facilitate the recovery. Security audits, penetration tests, constant updates of the softwares, scheduled backups, management of the privileges, and even biometric security should be standards in resilient infrastructure. A series of guidelines should be provided to all people that use an electronic device connected to the network of the infrastructure, and above all there's the need to make sure that these are enforced. Who runs the infrastructure shall have in mind that every electronic device is a potential point of access for an attacker. But this is not simple. The need for resilience comes in fact from how the threat of a cyber attack is perceived from the high management levels of an infrastructure or a government agency. Generally, from 2010 onwards, the paradigm of cybersecurity for critical infrastructures shifted from the concern of the sole risk of attacks coming from outside the network, to the fact that the attacks can come from the inside, through an infected flashdrive for example, as Stuxnet showed.

The perception of the threat is still a discriminant factor in how an infrastructure is protected. In the end, the responsibility of an attack falls on who runs the infrastructures whether this is a large-scale national critical infrastructure in the energy sector or a small scale bio-laboratory. Nevertheless, as the examples showed, today the risk of being attacked involves a wide range of actors and all of them should be somewhat prepared.

Assuming that an infrastructure takes all the measures depicted above, will it be resilient then? Being able to **prevent** cyberattacks is not an easy task. Penetration tests, privileges management, awareness raising in all the users of electronic devices of the infrastructures (advices like not bringing personal USB sticks to work, use difficult passwords and not revealing them to anyone, for examples) are the basis in preventing an attack. But we should take into account that the major attacks of the last three years used zero-day exploits. In that case infrastructures couldn't have prevented the attack, but they could have limited the consequences. Because preventing a zero-day exploit is impossible. Being prepared for something you don't know it is like creating a vaccine for a deadly virus that doesn't exist yet. Of course the attacks using zero-day exploits are borderline cases, since they are not available to everyone due to their high value and to the fact that they are kept only inside small circles of hackers. **Deterring** an attack is a pivotal move in a war that has in the cold war its main example. Given that a critical infrastructure does not have the power to retaliate, in this case showing to a potential enemy to be able to withstand or recover quickly from an attack decreases the chances that a particular enemy will attack you. The **detection** of an attack is another pillar of resilience. With a resilient infrastructure, with a well trained IT department the majority of the attacks could be detected and responded to. Without a resilient approach in case of an attack with a malware that uses a zero-day exploit, the history of events shows that years can pass before someone notices anything. As far as **response** is concerned, large scale infrastructures should be provided with an internal CERT (Computer Emergency Response Team), or be linked to a national CERT (engaging the public–private partnership) to ensure an appropriate response in terms of management and technical actions and coordination. As said above, a business continuity plan, penetration tests and contingency plans are essential to respond to a cyberattack without interrupting the activities of the infrastructure. Hypothetically, if the Natanz nuclear facility respected the characteristics above, it wouldn't have been infected by Stuxnet because no infected USB would have been inserted in the internal network. And if the attack would have come from outside, the infection would have taken place (since Stuxnet used four zero-day exploits), but recovery would have taken less. Still, trying to examine this "what if" scenarios is difficult because a lot of variables take place during an attack, but we can see an efficient aspect in the fact that, after being attacked, the Iranian infrastructures increased their defenses and resilience.

International Approaches on Resilience

On February 7th 2013, the "Cybersecurity Strategy of the European Union: an Open, Safe, and Secure Cyberspace" was presented through a press conference with the important remarks of Catherine Ashton· EU high representative, Neelie Kroes· Vice-President of the European Commission responsible for the Digital Agenda and Cecilia Malmström, EU Commissioner for Home Affairs. The remarks revolve around the fact that we rely on cyberspace in almost every sector of our lives, and thus the importance of defending it from cyberattacks. Neelie Kroes underlines one of the critical point of the EU Strategy, that's to say cyber resilience: "We need to protect our networks and systems, and make them resilient. That can only happen when all actors play their part and take up their responsibilities. Cyber threats are not contained to national borders: nor should cybersecurity be. So our strategy is accompanied by a proposed Directive to strengthen cyber-resilience within our single market. It will ensure companies take the measures needed for safe, stable networks. [...] Europe needs resilient systems and networks. Failing to act would impose significant costs: on consumers, on businesses, on society. A single cyber incident can cost from tens of thousands of euros for a small business—to millions for a large-scale data breach. Yet the majority of them could be prevented just by users taking simple and cheap measures."

In the document "Cybersecurity Strategy of the European Union: an Open, Safe and Secure Cyberspace", achieving cyber resilience is the first of the five strategic priorities of the EU to efficiently tackle cyberthreats. The pivotal factor for achieving a status of resilience for critical infrastructure is promoting Public–Private Partnership and collaboration. The additional factor is that EU could permit further security, in cases of threats with transnational characteristics, also coordinating a collective response. For these reasons the mandate of the European Network and Information Security Agency (ENISA) is being strengthened and modernized. In order to try and close the gap among Member States, the strategy of the European Union is associated with a proposal of legislation, that aims at setting for example "common minimum requirements for Network and Information Security (NIS) at national level which would oblige Member States to: designate national competent authorities for NIS and set up a well-functioning Computer Emergency Response Team [that would coordinate with the] Computer Emergency Response Team responsible for the security of the IT systems of the EU institutions, agencies and bodies ("CERT-EU") [that] was permanently established in 2012" The strategy stresses the importance of the Public–Private engagement as a paramount step, given the fact that most of the infrastructures are property of, and operated by, private bodies. On the other hand, from the private point of view, it is necessary to raise awareness on the risks of cyberthreats and establishing a risk management culture, in order to make the network and the information systems of a given infrastructure resilient.

The infrastructures' owners should also share information with the national NIS authorities and report any incident, in the same way that US infrastructures report to the US-CERT. One mean to foster the Public–Private Partnership could be the European Public–Private Partnership for Resilience (EP3R), that is a platform for public–private cooperation "on the identification of key assets, resources, functions and baseline requirements for resilience as well as cooperation needs and mechanisms to respond to large-scale disruptions affecting electronic communications". The last two aspects that the strategy reviews are the financial support for critical infrastructures, that would come from the Connecting Europe Facility (CEF) and the organization of cyber incident exercises at EU level, after the Cyber Europe 2010 and 2012 the second one included also the private sector.

On December 6th 2012, the Council of the European Union has released the Document "Proposal for a Council decision establishing the Specific Programme implementing Horizon 2020—The Framework Programme for Research and Innovation (2014–2020)" In this document, attention is devoted to the subject of Security in general and Cyber security in particular, listed as one specific theme of research.

The Financial Times of January 30th 2013 gives a good taste of the physical and cyber threats that the energy infrastructures will have to face in the next years. The time span of H2020 will be characterized from an increasing complexity and uncertainty, with consequent increase in the vulnerability of Critical Infrastructures. The conventional approach on risk management, based on a "a priori" classification of all the potential risks is not sufficient any more. "Think about unthinkable" is becoming a mandatory strategy in the field of Critical Infrastructure Protection (CIP). These new dimensions of the CIP require a new approach to resilience, going well beyond the past approach to fortress.

On 12th February 2013, the President of the United States, Barack Obama issued an Executive Order entitled "Improving Critical Infrastructure Cybersecurity", which has similar contents and measures to those included in the Cybersecurity strategy of the European Union.

Undoubtedly, this is a sign of how an important challenge the cybersecurity of Critical Infrastructures—and of their ICS—is becoming in different contexts.

A key tension that stems from the economic versus national security debate is the tension between the forces that are driving infrastructure modernisation (economic stimulus) vis-à-vis the forces that are demanding critical infrastructure protection. The discussion around Critical Infrastructures and the so-called "smart grids"—electric grids based on ICT—is emblematic. Thus, a potential 'modernisation' agenda is brought into direct conflict with a security agenda. The policy intervention that a government uses to meet the needs of the nation must be carefully balanced to heighten security without creating barriers to innovation, economic growth, and the free flow of information. To find the right equilibrium between innovation and security will be one of the major challenge in the time span of H2020.

Bibliography

B. Abolghasem, IAEA Report: The growing resilience of Iran's nuclear program (Foreign Policy J., 2012), http://www.foreignpolicyjournal.com/2012/02/27/iaea-report-the-growing-resilienc e-of-irans-nuclear-program/. Accessed 5 May 2013

M. Ahlers, Inside a government computer attack exercise (CNN, 2011), http://edition.cnn.com/ 2011/10/17/tech/innovation/cyberattack-exercise-idaho/index.html. Accessed 5 May 2013

A. Klimburg (ed.), National cyber security framework manual (NATO CCD COE publication, 2012), http://www.ccdcoe.org/publications/books/NationalCyberSecurityFrameworkManual. pdf. Accessed 5 May 2013

C. Ashton, Press conference on the launch of the EU's cyber security strategy (2013), http://www. consilium.europa.eu/uedocs/cms_Data/docs/pressdata/EN/foraff/135287.pdf. Accessed 5 May 2013

C. Malmström, Stepping up the fight against cybercriminals to secure a free and open internet (Press conference on the launch of the EU's cyber security strategy, 2013), http://europa.eu/ rapid/press-release_SPEECH-13-105_en.htm. Accessed 5 May 2013

G. Chazan, Cyber saboteurs stalk the oil industry (Financial Times, 2013), http://www.ft.com/ cms/s/0/989aa68c-692e-11e2-b254-00144feab49a.html#axzz2Y5HyNmEC. Accessed 5 May 2013

European Commission, Proposal for a regulation of the European parliament and of the council establishing horizon 2020—The framework programme for research and innovation

(2014–2020) (European Commission, 2011), http://ec.europa.eu/research/horizon2020/pdf/ proposals/com(2011)_809_final.pdf. Accessed on 5 May 2013

European Commission, Cybersecurity strategy of the European Union: an open, safe and secure cyberspace (Euopean Commission, 2013), http://ec.europa.eu/dgs/home-affairs/e-library/ documents/policies/organized-crime-and-human-trafficking/cybercrime/docs/join_2013_1_ en.pdf. Accessed 5 May 2013

D. Goldman, Hacker hits on U.S. power and nuclear targets spiked in 2012 (CNN, 2013), http:// money.cnn.com/2013/01/09/technology/security/infrastructure-cyberattacks/index.html. Accessed 5 May 2013

G. Gritsai et al., Scada safety in numbers. Positive technologies ed. (2013), http://www.ptsecurity .com/download/SCADA_analytics_english.pdf. Accessed 5 May 2013

Idaho National Laboratories, Vulnerability analysis of energy delivery control systems (US DOE publication, 2011), http://energy.gov/sites/prod/files/Vulnerability%20Analysis%20of%20 Energy%20Delivery%20Control%20Systems%202011.pdf. Accessed 5 May 2013

N. Kroes, Using cybersecurity to promote European values. Press conference on the launch of the EU's cyber security strategy (2013), http://europa.eu/rapid/press-release_SPEECH-13-104_en.htm. Accessed May 5 2013

NERC, Cyber attack task force final report (NERC, 2012), http://www.nerc.com/ docs/cip/catf/12-CATF_Final_Report_BOT_clean_Mar_26_2012-Board%20Accepted%20 0521.pdf. Accessed 5 May 2013

Newsroom, Iran 'fends off new Stuxnet cyber attack (BBC, 2012), http://www.bbc.co.uk/news/ world-middle-east-20842113. Accessed 5 May 2013

B. Obama, Improving critical infrastructure cybersecurity—executive order (White House press office, 2013), http://www.whitehouse.gov/the-press-office/2013/02/12/executive-order-improving-critical-infrastructure-cybersecurity. Accessed 5 May 2013

P. Paganini, The importance of security requirements in design of SCADA systems (PenTest auditing and standards, 2012:06)

D. Sanger, Obama order sped up wave of cyberattacks against Iran (The New York Times, 2012), http://www.nytimes.com/2012/06/01/world/middleeast/obama-ordered-wave-of-cyberat-tacks-against-iran.html?pagewanted=all&_r=0. Accessed 5 May 2013

SHODAN Search Engine (2009), http://www.shodanhq.com/. Accessed 5 May 2013

US Department of Homeland Security: Common cybersecurity vulnerabilities in indus-trial control systems (2011), http://ics-cert.us-cert.gov/sites/default/files/DHS_ Common_Cybersecurity_Vulnerabilities_ICS_2010.pdf. Accessed 5 May 2013

US Department of Homeland Security: ICS–CERT incident response summary report 2009–2011 (2011), http://scadahacker.com/library/Documents/ICS_Events/ICS-CERT%20Incident%20 Response%20Summary%20Report.pdf. Accessed 5 May 2013

US Department of Homeland Security: ICS–CERT monthly monitor Oct–Dec 2012 (2011), http://ics-cert.us-cert.gov/pdf/ICS-CERT_Monthly_Monitor_Oct-Dec2012.pdf. Accessed 5 May 2013

US National Communication Systems: Technical information bulletin 04-1, supervisory con-trol and data acquisition (SCADA) systems (2004), http://www.ncs.gov/library/tech_ bulletins/2004/tib_04-1.pdf. Accessed 5 May 2013

N. Weinstein, Stuxnet attacks Iran again, reports say (CNET, 2012), http://news.cnet.com/8301-1009_3-57560799-83/stuxnet-attacks-iran-again-reports-say/. Accessed 5 May 2013

J. Weiss, Assuring industrial control system (ICS) cyber security. CSIS ed. (2008), http://csis.org/ files/media/csis/pubs/080825_cyber.pdf. Accessed 5 May 2013

K. Zetter, Vulnerability lets hackers control building locks, electricity, elevators and more (Wired US, 2013), http://www.wired.com/threatlevel/2013/02/tridium-niagara-zero-day/?utm_ source=feedburner&utm_medium=feed&utm_campaign=Feed%253A+wired27b+%2528 Wired%253A+Blog+-+Threat+Level%2529. Accessed on 5 May 2013